Jim Fargiano

The Spoken
Words
of Spirit

Lessons From The Other Side

Outskirts Press, Inc.
Denver, Colorado

Outskirts Press, Inc.
http://www.outskirtspress.com

ISBN: 978-1-4327-2080-3

Outskirts Press and the "OP" logo are trademarks belonging to Outskirts Press, Inc.

PRINTED IN THE UNITED STATES OF AMERICA

DEDICATION

To my mother, Gerri, and father, Tony.
If it wasn't for their physical presence
I never would have been given the opportunity
to enter into this life. They enabled me
to have the experiences that created this book.

FOREWORD

Where can two worlds collide and have the outcome feel comforting and peaceful? It would be in our everyday existence, where God and Spirit accompany us during our daily journeys throughout our activities, **throughout our lives**. With their assistance and subtle reassurances, we as physical beings are helped to achieve our lessons in life, whether those lessons are to be learned on a soul basis or of the material world. I have come to understand through seemingly countless hours of channeling and meditation that as soon as we think we have Spirit figured out, we are taught something completely new.

INTRODUCTION

It is my intent to allow you to read about some of the wonderful thoughts of wisdom that Spirit has enabled me to have the privilege of receiving. From the first day that I knew I was able to channel, I have been mostly delighted by the messages and significance of them, both large and small. It is through the constant education in interpretation of imagery that Spirit has brought forth to me that has kept my connection with the souls from the other side both fun and frustrating. This continually leaves me searching for more answers and knowledge of what it means to be part of an existence that most people have merely scratched the surface in understanding. Where, why, how, and who are words that have become a very strong part of my thought process; however, the most personally agitating question I am left with after meditation or channeling someone's loved one is, when.

What I have found is that no matter how dire we deem something to be on the earth plane, those on the other side very often run on their own timeline. One of the key elements that I know is being taught is for all of us to be patient with our requests and prayers to all those who now reside on the other side of the divide. We are by no means alone in this world. Our family and friends continue to survive through an energy that is omnipotent. After all, we have been created in the image of God, and if He is the truth in what everlasting life is, then without question, we are too.

In the following pages, excerpts and complete transcripts of channeled messages from Spirit will afford you the opportunity to think and expand your mind and your consciousness. This is one of the primary attempts of our friends to teach us that **we are not limited by anything in this world, with the exception of our own minds**. Hopefully, you will find this book to be helpful to you on many levels.

A great number of these messages should help you to understand how to cope with the loss of loved ones, with the changing relationships we all undergo, and most assuredly, they will teach you how to see life more for its magnificent splendor and optimistic meanings. We have a duty as an extension of God to be and act in the highest and most positive and pure way we can. In a sense, many of the words that will follow in this book can be seen as a simplified process in which to learn to enjoy and behold the privilege of life that our Creator has given us. You will see through the ease in which they speak to us that our souls never die.

Certainly, without question, my own evolution in this most physical world has been greatly enhanced and changed in many ways since God and Spirit saw it fit to have me "open" to receive messages. My perspective on life and the unseen miracles and joys that went by unnoticed before are always being highlighted. Time after time, I see the hand of Spirit at work.

Perhaps I would never have been given this experience if it were not for one of my good friends, John Klumpp. He introduced me to a book named *Creative Visualizations* during a very tumultuous time in my life. After giving me specific instructions not to worry about reading the sections on meditation because he knew "it wasn't my style," he told me to try out some of the relaxation techniques. John thought these would be helpful in putting me in a less stressed attitude and approach towards the negativity that swirled around me. Little did he, or I, know that this simple gesture would change my life in such a dramatic way.

I had always thought I would be on a fast track to success. At that time, it was only seen in my mind's eye and in my heart that I would always become a successful entrepreneur. There were not many thoughts of Spirit in my general scope of philosophies, although many times, I would find myself silently praying for help and guidance and generally expecting that it would come. From the time I was a young boy, I found an interest in amassing money and prosperity. What I didn't know then was that I was already using the art of visualization to make this a reality. My family grew up in modest surroundings, and with my three siblings, my parents did their best to make ends meet. This was also one of the catalysts to have me crave for something easier and financially stronger for my future. It just seemed that they were all afraid to think "big" in what they saw for the future. Somehow, the logic was that it would prevent us from feeling disappointed if nothing good came. The other outcome was that I started to accept that it was fine just to survive. Without disrespecting my family, I wanted to find a way out of that concept and onto a path that would leave me feeling freer about enjoying life's attractions.

My life was moving faster than most of my friends' lives. I skipped my last year of high school and went to a community college, where I was just as bored with the intended education. This was a problem for me throughout most of my school years. My time was more consumed with the business I had than it was with focusing on the college curriculum. After that first year, my attention was devoted to business-related issues only.

It was also an era in which my personal relationship was progressing. At nineteen, against what I now know was a strong spiritual message, I got married. My first house was purchased two years later, and two years after that, my first child was born. My son, Chris, was a gift in my mind, and we are still extremely close today. My beautiful daughter, Justina, was born two and a half years later and still holds a special place in my heart. The business I started was excelling, but then, the stress and underhanded behavior that my now ex-wife was putting me through basically shredded everything I had been working for. This, without a doubt, put me into quite a depression, which is why my good friend, John, handed me the book that allowed me to change my life and direction. In a most unusual way, the person who made my life unbearable was indirectly responsible for giving me the chance to reach the point in which my life went from broken to suddenly being spiritually blessed. It is another lesson that isn't lost on me as I continue to work with Spirit. What also helped was the fact that I have no ill feelings towards any of the problems from that point in my life.

After immediately being "led" to the first meditation in the book, without delay, many in spirit blitzed me with images. I went to my friend's house afterward and asked him what he thought the images I had seen meant to him. John looked at me as though I were crazy and after listening to him, I did begin to wonder if perhaps the stress I was under had actually made my mind snap. For some unexplained reason that I now know was Spirit, I went back to the book a couple of days later. This time when I tried to meditate, I "felt" something change within me. It wasn't until much later that I would see a visual image of a massive beam of white light entering into the top of my head that allowed me to have a better, if not still confused, understanding of what had been transpiring. Even today, I see this intense light whenever I am looking to validate that I am at least trying to follow the level of lessons and directions Spirit is trying to get me to move through.

For weeks after, I would spend hours upon hours in John's house following this initial indoctrination. We would also spend time during the evening going for long walks while all of this unfolded. I'd channel messages and directives from Spirit that were given to me to follow. Many times, it felt like I was being educated, similar to some sort of condensed college course. There is no simple explanation as to how easy it was for me to get images, whether they were literally visual or subtle impressions in my mind. John would take notes on everything that came through. Somehow, I thought in the future I would refer to them, but when I pulled them out to look at them for the purpose of this book, they were completely illegible and the pencil was mostly nonexistent. This is something that I find to be typical of Spirit. It is not always what I think is best or easiest, it is what *they know* is best.

As days passed during that span of time, I was led, or introduced, to several people who I feel helped mold and guide my newfound ability. Without the initial encouragement of Marguerite Abramo and Patty Gang, I may not have pursued the avenue in which my spiritual growth and recognition soared. I met Marguerite through John and subsequently, she introduced me to Patty, who for a long time gave me both practical and spiritual knowledge about a great deal of what I was encountering.

Through these two friends, I was led to a metaphysical church and was befriended by a minister, as well as medium, Ginnie Berg. This giving lady was patient with all my questions and very informative in laying a foundation of accepted interpretations of many of the images I was seeing, but didn't know how to interpret. Until recently, she was still doing some wonderful work through her own church, *A Sanctuary of Infinite Spirit,* and even now, I still occasionally pick her brain for guidance.

I would be remiss in not thanking Annette Cannariato for all she has meant and done for me. My relationship with her has ranged from business associate to friend to confidant and then into a much more meaningful and loving connection. She has served as my secretary, partner, planner, and in general, has made my life as easy and stress free as it could possibly be. There are no words to fully express her importance to me on a multitude of levels. She is an example of Spirit putting the right person in my life at the right time and is a shining star and constant reminder to me that this world does have some great and truly extraordinary people. Through my progression as a medium, Annette has been a catalyst of support and has given me just the right amount of push when she sees me starting to lose focus on what I am supposed to be doing in this lifetime. She has done her best to help me fulfill the lessons and mission Spirit seems to want me to follow.

My connection to her helped me to maintain a feeling of normalcy. I was still deeply involved with my own office supply business, but felt my need to be there dwindling as I opened more and more to the connection to God and the messages from the Light. For years now, I have been trying to comprehend the vastness of this privileged communication. At the same time, I'm trying to understand the simplicity of it too. This created an unfair burden on Annette to try to fill a lot of my responsibilities to the store, but finally because of economic hardships and other situations out of my control, the company was closed. This has left me with more time to ponder my future and to listen to some compelling messages from many high-level beings in spirit.

Simply finding the time and overcoming problems associated with the writing of this book has allowed me to mention another person who has become a vital cog in assisting my pilgrimage. Maureen Schmidt has developed as rapidly as I have and is now someone I lean on for comparative messages, as well as to completely aid me with the prayer and meditation group that was created years ago—without my knowledge, initially. For me, it is comforting to have someone to go to just in order to see if she picks things up the way I do or if she might have an alternative interpretation of the same symbol. Maureen has great things planned for her by Spirit. Her beautiful daughter, Chrisy, who is in the kingdom of God, also works periodically as a source of information and a guide for myself too.

The group I refer to had its base in my friend John's home. It originally was he and I getting information from Spirit, then our friend Marguerite joined us and after that, Patty. As people began to find out about the channeling I was doing, the ebb and flow of physical bodies became too burdensome for his living room. Subsequently, I was forced to move the prayer and meditation meeting to Main Street, where it has excelled for over a decade now. Many people have come, stayed for a meeting, a month of meetings, or years, and then drifted away. During its infancy, Spirit spoke of having a core group to retain; however, human nature and demands on people in the physical world have limited it to a loyal handful of attendees, all of whom I consider important friends. Whether they know it or not, I feel an imbalance when one of them is missing.

The imbalance of energy is something that I will always wonder about. How could I be so connected at times, and then feel an absolute void when someone is missing? It goes further than that, too. Some days, I awake so confident that the readings or healings I may do that day will come easily and smoothly, yet, there are other days that, admittedly, I put myself into a quandary of worry that the messages won't be strong enough. It took me years to recognize that the ups and downs I feel simply don't have anything to do with my ability to connect. Instead, it is easier for me to see that whoever is sitting in front of me may intentionally, or unintentionally, be causing what I see as a blockage. Most of the time, it leaves me physically exhausted and mentally frustrated.

I have not figured out why someone would come to sit with me with the intent of trying to trip me up or purposely lie about what is coming through from Spirit. Even though I'm still not comfortable with those situations, I am stubbornly learning that the loss is on their end and not mine. Maybe it is supposed to be a lesson for both of us. This is one area that I don't think I'll ever understand or be content about.

A lot of people have asked me if every day is fun and exciting as a medium, but the truth is that there have been many times when I find myself in depressed funks or confused states of mind and direction. The frustration in understanding the numerous messages I am given during readings with clients, as well as in my everyday issues, never seem to stop. The fact is that I am my own worst enemy and critic, as I want to be perfect in deciphering the images and not letting anyone feel that I have misinformed them. Some of my friends get a kick out of how paranoid I become if I don't think I got the translation right in certain situations.

It might be important for you to know that no matter how easy any medium or psychic may make message-giving seem, there is an internal learning process that is always ongoing. This was the case right from the first time I connected with the other side. Of course, the biggest question I had was, "Why me?" In my mind, I wasn't someone special and never saw myself as being anything other than just the average person. Being blessed with the ability to communicate with the other side was a privilege, and I couldn't come to terms easily with why I was selected to have this gift. I was not reading or trying to incorporate any sense of spirituality into my life any more than it was. Until about six months prior to my opening, my thoughts of mediums and psychics was of such a nature that I knew there was "something" that these people connected with, but until I could see it for myself, I thought I would always be skeptical. For me, seeing, sensing, and hearing everything more than adequately proved the availability of the other side.

One of the earliest messages I received for myself was of one of my spiritual guides telling me that they were aware of my utterance from when I was four years old. I was told that this was the first time I thought that I would like to be able to heal people "just like Jesus did." This was a revelation to me in terms of only my youthful age. Many times, while sitting in church with my family, the only stories or sermons that held my interest were those in which the priest or minister were speaking about the physical healings performed by Christ. The ability to do this was intriguing in my mind, and I would daydream about having the "power" to simply lay my hands on someone with a severe illness and watch them be restored to perfect health. This dream is now reality in many ways.

Since the beginning of this new transition of personal and spiritual development, I have steadfastly tried to adhere and administer to each and every one of Spirit's messages and directives. It has not always been easy because oftentimes, I find myself in conflict with the focus and purpose of their words. Although I'm not trying to be obstinate, there seems to be a part of me that wants to know more than ever that I am in control of my own destiny. The free will that God gave us actually enables each of us to do just that. However, through my experiences, it seems that most of us only invoke it for situations that lead us to something not quite as rewarding than if we followed the guidance of Spirit. Our lives would be so much easier if we all had reverent trust in the High Powers and took the advice that comes through in varying forms. We all can sense more than most of us give ourselves credit for.

In talking with numerous clients, it is abundantly obvious that virtually every one of us on this great planet have had a clairsentient experience. This ability to understand and read our "gut instincts," or "women's intuition," is truly an attempt from our loved ones who have passed over, or a higher source, trying to lead us in the right direction. It is a connection to a presence that is different than anything we have in our physical realm. It may come in as a forewarning of something to come in our life that we would probably look at as a negative event. The truth is that Spirit is trying their best to allow us the time to make changes or make the right preparations for the episode. If the feeling doesn't scare us into inaction, then we are able to take advantage of the time coming to either try to remedy the situation or come to peace with it in our own minds. It is vital to remember that we are nothing more than an esoteric energy housed in a physical body, trying to live in the reality of this world that was created by others.

Many of my clients ask if communication with Spirit physically drains me. After years of having contact with the other side, I have to give a resounding "yes" to that question. For the first couple of years, the ability to chat with Spirit came as a big lift in my energy level, although my physical condition had almost immediately become a problem and remains that way with the writing of this book. As the years have passed, the toll it has taken on me is quite obvious. My sleep patterns have been off in every conceivable manner. I seem to be hit with a wave of exhaustion and sometimes, dizziness, after my early-day sessions with people. My night appointments leave me feeling wired, even though I still feel tired. What I have learned from this is that frequently, my own physical ailments will closely mirror those of many of the people coming to see me. However, by having undergone so much myself, interpretation of what I see and feel becomes much easier.

Those in spirit have a delightful way of getting their point across to us. It is beyond any doubt that I see and have been told that all of our loved ones who have passed to the other side continue to retain the personality they had in life. Of course, they learn about all the choices and decisions that were made in err on this side and are taught how to correct and make amends for any and all people who they may have hurt. Several times over, a loving Spirit will tell me about their duty to enhance their soul by coming to recognize the improper way they may have done something while in their physical world.

I have had sessions when someone in the spiritual realm will come through to speak to a loved one, whether it is a child or spouse, and not only be visually focused on having me relay abhorrent behavior, but will begin to unravel a tale of abuse. Some of the most heartwarming and healing messages can come from the very people who created havoc in our personal lives. Most of these types have made it clear to me that they have been taught and shown all the mistakes they made while they lived in the physical world, and then advised how to adjust and make amends for them.

For myself, I have found the daily incantations of Spirit to be the most informative. This doesn't mean that it is without some cryptic coding, oftentimes leaving me more puzzled then not. These messages are frequently mirrored during the nights I have our prayer, meditation, and channeling group. A lot of the excerpts you will be reading are verbatim from the transcripts I keep. Most of the time, Spirit is simply trying to teach and lead us in learning how to be and live a more positive and productive life.

THE WORDS BEGIN,
THE LESSONS BEGIN

What will follow are some of the more "mainstream" prayers, messages and invocations that are periodically given. In addition to these, sometimes Spirit likes to give phrases or anecdotal messages for all of us to think about. These seem to be the only times when I know their intent is to be somewhat mysterious because it forces us to evaluate and think about what the message behind the words actually is. I find that the interpretation will vary from one person to the next, thus, highlighting the fact that there is, and will always be, more than one way to view the words of God and Spirit.

We must all remember that the only thing constant in the universe is change.

That line came into my head as I sat here perplexed by my lack of understanding of the passing into Spirit of my son's friend in an unfortunate occurrence. While I thought I was asking questions to myself—something that isn't possible because God and Spirit are always listening—this quickly given sentence actually helped to remind me that not all things are in our control. My son and I were in my friend's home late in the evening, watching all the rescue boats and helicopters try to locate this sixteen-year-old boy, not knowing at the time that it was his friend who had capsized in the cold March waters. Spirit was giving me messages, not of exact location, but of his seemingly slow, physical passing into the blissful world of Eternal Life. I was frustrated that this person was only within a few hundred yards of where I was sitting; yet no information was given to help expedite finding him.

Understanding that we, as humans, cannot interfere with someone's destiny unless Spirit allows it, is exactly what I took from this one sentence: *We must all remember that the only thing constant in the universe is change.* The sentence isn't new, but it did give new meaning to me. Over the years that I have been channeling messages, many times I am taught, and re-taught, that we have limited resources on this level. It is what we do with them that makes a difference. Are we to idly stand by as negativity that surrounds us takes hold of all things, or is it our choice and destiny to limit it as much as possible? What good can come from a young man's death? Can we take this loss and educate other young people of the importance of thinking in a forward time frame rather than just the "now" aspect that most of us see? Surely, God doesn't expect us to live our lives grieving and depressed. We must take a negative and turn it into a positive. That is the only way for everyone to have a better understanding of right versus wrong.

The other side has always been very quick to transmit a sentence or phrase for us to think about. Some of them are easy to decipher, others are more camouflaged in their meaning. They might be given for the moment or for us to retain for a lifetime. The following are four short messages given to me during one of my meditations. I was asking for Spirit to enlighten me further about what seems at times to be too short a physical life for some people. Amongst other more private pieces of information were these:

Those who are left behind in the physical world as attrition is created around them become stronger if their hearts allow it.

Death can be the most awesome time of life when guided through natural fate and destiny.

Intensity rings the soul, but life lets it shine. Feel the power within.

Seclusion leads to confusion. Be social and life's inequities will seem insignificant.

While sitting and reflecting on Easter night, 2001, Spirit asked me to sit at the keyboard and create music through their words. Obliging, this is what I heard on this widely held, sacred day:

Though there have been years of endurance and silence from the flock of God, it is time that the

Abernathy of success sings the graces of His high thoughts. Allow all men and women the courage to reign supreme in a world that has become one of such cynicism by uniting in trust and faith. Share with the masses of His children that the Lord is alive and well and that no fear should ever leave any of His flesh in a foothold of confusion and despair. It is the absolution of all sins that makes your High Energy the only true and comforting force in an environment that preaches vast differences in what the words of the great masters have been translated into. God has worked hard to resurrect life back into the souls of all mankind. Trust the simplicity of the message and let the Light shine from within your souls and be seen as **love** coming out from your hearts.

*   *   *   *   *   *

Thinking about these words and their apparent depth is perhaps the best place for us to share the journey of a spiritual path. Even as I finish this section, my knowledge of exactly what this book will mean to you, the readers, is as mystifying to me as it was when I knowingly connected with Spirit for the first time.

Wherever possible, I will let you know which Spirit has given me the words you will be reading. Keep in mind that even I don't always know where or who this wisdom is coming from. I will do my best to write exactly what I understand from Spirit. This may cause some of the writings to seem like they are in the third person form at times. Even within the same paragraph, it is possible to be reading it in the "I" version in context, then in the "you" form. Spirit wants us to think, and at the same time, know that they are part of us at all times. The following is the bulk of a message received during a fairly recent, deep meditation, where I was taken into an astral projection.

*   *   *   *   *   *

The Light shines upon the magnificent. All those entrusted with the intensity and power from the God Being should adjoin together and amass a great outflow of humanitarian, as well as, evolutionary actions. In other words, we are looking for those who have been given the creation of Light, the gift of Light, to stand forth and to communicate, regardless of the communication type. It can be words on paper; it can be well-documented orations, or one person, one thought, and one project at a time.

The greatness that this country was founded on has been shaken. The disciples of those who wrote and forecast the future with the documentation of the Declaration of Independence and the Constitution are **all people**. As a mass society, it is vital for you as an individual to stand tall, proud, and brave in the face of adversity and dysfunction for those who do not understand the peaceful intent of the Highest Power.

It is up to each and every one of you to wrap yourself in a Light and way that makes you feel safe. I come to you and through you, not with devilish intentions or demonic accusations, but I come to you instead with the wisdom, with the courage, with the fortitude of all those in power on the side of Christ. You must undoubtedly stand tall for the environment and stand tall for your environment. We can no longer desecrate the "barren" lands that are full of life and content. To the lower kingdom of plants and animals, they are full of life—their life.

We can no longer stand by and witness the atrocities of distrust and hatred on all levels. We are a powerful being and you are entrusted and enveloped in an energy that will forever embolden you to carry a message to hold the torch high, to ignite a movement within people, to return to the basic fundamentals of spiritual philosophies and beliefs. You—everyone—must take the time to let compassion rise high within your souls, high within your minds, and forever be content with the gift of abundance, excitement, and enlightenment.

We preach from the side of Christ in an effort to have each and every one of you abandon negative thoughts and abandon an attitude that has been repetitious in nature to many people; that attitude being, "It does not make a difference." You will see that it does make a difference. Compassion and love and a free flow of it are what bring peace to the world. Power is the pulpit that needs to be addressed. Those in power must have an understanding that the attitudes that are buffeting the common goodwill are what will destroy this great planet. I need for everyone to think about this. I need for the seas to ravage civilization, for the winds to pound down attitudes of evil, attitudes of indifference, attitudes of ill will towards their fellow man. It is feared that only then will mankind embrace the depth of happiness and complete humanity that God seeks for them.

It is important for all people to understand that those who accumulate material wealth should do so in a way that is not disparaging or demeaning to anyone who crosses their path. We have told you in the past that material wealth and abundance were part of the Master's planned Creation. The Creation, our Creator in a sense, has entrusted to each of you a great avenue in which you can reach success. Most of you do not ever find the path. Some of you do.

Some of you do not understand what is directly in front of you. It is just as simple as a pump that can take water and push it against the grain, against gravity. There is a situation where the wings of eagles and wings of angels are readily available to try to open the path of security. You must take the security that you begin to receive and you must share it and spread it to those facets and organizations that are trying to create the strength and power of the spiritual being.

You cannot do it alone, and we understand that, but alone and alone and alone, united together, creates a distinction of power, a landslide of activity, a uniqueness of the word of God and more than anything else, that leads to action. Action is progress. Progress is simply putting into motion the words of enlightenment, the gift of God, as well as the everlasting and all eternal beautification of all souls, all the time. Do not fear being ridiculed for being of a different mind. In the beginning, upon the existence of the first human being, the plurality of thoughts was not to look at things as being situated in what has become today's mantra of, "What's in it for me?" I say that from the side of Spirit with virtually the same question—what is in it for us? Why is it that we, in spirit, will continue to pound and hound all of you to reach the pinnacle of success, the apex of understanding, as well as the paragon of pulchritude, which is life itself?

When you go forward from this day and from tomorrow and all the tomorrows after, you must analyze your actions. Is what you are doing helpful to anyone or is it a hindrance? Is being dismissive of love and life helping just you, or do you think it is helping others? Can you understand how opening to the Love and Light can be helpful to yourself and to all others?

This is the word I bring you. I, as Saint Paul, am a prophet. I am also a leader, an explorer, and an expander. I walked in the time of the Master Jesus and I shared His word. His work came directly from the highest source of Light. You now have the same source available to you. You now have the same source available to you. I can continue to repeat that, but only until you find in your hearts and souls the strength and courage and the will to fight forward, to fight procrastination, and to fight those of evil intent, will you ever live up to your fullest and most important energy. Many of you can already walk with your heads held high; others, though, need to be reprimanded.

The earth must be torn apart to some degree to create a new wave of realization and a new wave of fearless foreboding and a new wave of snatching out the quality of life that each and every being deserves. There should be no cast system anywhere. Men should be equal to women; women should be equal to men. People of dark skin are no better or no worse than those of white, yellow, or the proverbial redskin. Those with eyes shaped differently are just as empowered as those who have wide eyes. Those who believe in the tradition and faith of a certain religion should not be persecuted because they are trying to follow the word of God and Christ. They should be heard. Part of the problem in the way we see society today is that throughout civilization, tolerance, patience, and the willingness to forgive others' beliefs has gone by the wayside.

I, as Saint Paul, am asking for each of you to adorn yourself with the protection of the Light, to create a haven of safety and of trust. It is my intent to get each of you to open to the brilliance of powerful, loving relationships, but to digest it for the truth of what it is and not for the truth of what you want it to be. Pure love comes with no added efforts. Pure love comes with a shared enjoyable equality in the way you both see life. Relationships are based not only on differences, but the good relationships are based on friendships and the fact that you need not rescue everyone from their delusional thoughts and dysfunctional ways because in the end, if you try to do that, you become delusional and dysfunctional yourself.

We are embarking on a period of time from now to and through 2012, where the earth changes will continue to ravage certain parts of not only this country, but all over the world. God has seen fit not to have His wrath shine, but to have your compassion shine. What can you do to help your fellow man or woman? What can you do to embrace the fears of a child and to alleviate the stresses that this society has now become? All people must honor the earth. You must learn to utilize the normal powers without abusing that which creates fuel and energy. A walk or a ride on a bike is just as powerful as anything you can do to help the ecosystem. Quite simply, if you want the earth to survive, you must pray and pray some more.

In today's world, I understand speed is of the essence and perhaps more than anything, I am trying to get each of you to slow down, to think, to purify your thoughts, to embrace the Light. This will allow you to live freely and easily to such a great extent that fear is not part of who you are anymore and that you take away that fear from those who cannot protect themselves. I come with arms outspread from the pristine arena of life to ask each of you to open your minds and hearts to those who are in need, but also to open the minds and hearts **of** those in need. This will be done, as I have previously stated, in large masses, or simply as an audience of one. Perhaps that should be the mantra that you need to use for yourselves because even though there are billions of souls on this great planet Earth, the Great Power, those you see as your God, will continue to look at each person and soul as an individual. Your life counts. Your thoughts count. Your emotions count. Your security counts, and your prosperity truly counts.

*　　*　　*　　*　　*　　*

While I understood the basic premise of all of this, I was surprised that the message ended where it did. It was later explained to me that without a feeling of prosperity, most people are too uncomfortable to spend any of their assets on the mission work that Spirit seems to be pushing us to do. As I am prone to do, I questioned Spirit's use of the word "assets" and was abruptly told that our time, when spent in good use, is the most important asset we have, and it generally goes largely misused or misspent.

One of the things I recognized about this entire message was just how far my ability to interpret and understand what I see and hear has come. As I was looking through some old transcripts and teachings, I came across one from September of 1995. After reading it, I also realized just how vastly a decade could change things that were good into things that have become a target for ineptness. One of the voices I was hearing while I was reading this old message kept telling me that it should be included so that people can see what happens when we follow the basic tenets of good and moral thinking. Then you will be able to see, if you are aware at all of the media and news concerning the United Nations' "oil for food" scandal, what happens when greed enters man's mind and how it interferes with the true will of God's work. It is a mark of how easily all other years of good work can be overlooked.

THE EGYPTIAN—
SEPTEMBER 28, 1995

What I wish to discuss with all of you is the thought

of resiliency. Being able to bounce back is vital when you live a physical life. Time after time, you will be challenged, tempted, and tested by many situations. The type of test and where it comes from is totally unimportant. The way you respond to it, however, is of extreme urgency and optimum movements by yourself must be made. Meeting challenges afterwards should be done in very straightforward and direct, loving, but forceful ways. Some of you have fallen astray when changes have taken place in your own lives, and you have opted to focus on everyone but yourself.

Sometimes what we wish for you to focus on is your own stability, your own love, and the life that you nurture and have learned and allowed to grow since your inception back into the physical world. All I am asking is for you to just please keep your thoughts and intentions raised to the highest level and not to let negativity cascade upon you.

An example of resiliency is actually that of the United Nations. For half a century now, this organization has represented peace, or the will to be peaceful, in completion of this planet. Little is said about this unique organization. Much is gained, whether you realize it or not, by the constant work that takes place behind the walls of the house members of each nation. Ultimately, every individual country, regardless of how large or small, should be represented in this wonderful place. As they approach their birthday, more and more announcements will be sent forth by their leadership. This organization is one that is seldom looked at with the importance and reverence that it so deserves. I ask you to please simply take note of it and watch as the aggressiveness in which they pursue peace is brought to your attention.

Finally, it is important for you to know about the resiliency of Spirit and souls. We use the term "Spirit" over and over, but in actuality, we are referring to the souls on the God side of life. The "other side" of this invisible fence or wall is one in which learning takes place in great strides, love abounds endlessly, and understanding and knowledge are grasped at faster levels than when you are in the physical plane. Resiliency of the souls and the ability for them to constantly change to different situations is met over and over again, after each different incarnated lifetime. All I am trying to say is that understanding continues, even on what you consider to be the side of death. Learning and Love, Life, and Light, are all aspects of the spiritual world and these aspects are all heeded and understood with more intensity than you could ever imagine as you live through yet another learning lifetime.

*　　*　　*　　*　　*　　*

Ongoing messages from higher spirits to teach or encourage us to open more to the energies and powers of psychic ability and phenomena are frequent. The message that follows is an example of many I've received over the years. Mostly, even though the wording might be different from time to time, the gists of the lessons are the same. The following message was received through three of the spirits that I have channeled; however, on this one night, they all tried to convey the same thoughts.

EGYPTIAN, ONE FEATHER, AND KWAN YIN—

Egyptian—I wish to discuss with all of you shades of understanding psychic and spiritual phenomena. For many of you, there has been much frustration in opening psychically. This lesson is not so much a teaching of abilities, but more so a teaching of awareness. For those of you who have felt as though there is no breakthrough psychically, it is the understanding of Spirit that we wish to portray to you in a different light.

Energies are felt and utilized by virtually everyone. Those who feel as though they cannot see Spirit are amongst those who **feel** the strongest. What I mean by this is that you have gone through your lives with a knowing and an understanding of movements **before you have taken them**. This understanding comes in such a subtle way that you are unaware that you have tapped into Spirit. There is movement around each of you in multiples. While you all may have two, three, or four stationed spiritual leaders, tens and tens more flit around at the opportune times to assist.

Feeling itchiness in or around your temples may actually reflect a Spirit's desire to assist in an auditory opening. Pains around the forehead are generally recognition that clairvoyant abilities are being manipulated. All of these sensations are more readily noticeable, but what isn't are the internal "knowings."

The solar plexus chakra offers the easiest opening to Spirit. If you wish to call it "intuition," that is acceptable, but what you must truly understand is that this comes from tapping into the powers of a higher source. How many times have you been delayed when you are heading out to an affair or function for no apparent reason? How many times did someone call you or interrupt you when stepping out the door? All of these little synchronizations have been given to you as a way of communicating. In most cases, an earlier departure could have meant trouble would have happened down the line. It is one way the multitude of spirits are working to protect you.

Briefly, I will change the subject to clairvoyance. It is only as a means of contrasting the often felt and most misunderstood clairsentient energies. For most humans, the ability to see is the ability to believe. Swift images are given, but what happens even to the most clairvoyant person is that they begin to **feel** what they think they see. The images are actually not there. It is an adjustment for you to make again because Spirit finds it easier to work clairsentiently or through the energy center of the solar plexus rather than through the third eye. I bring this up not to upset anyone who does not have the ability to see Spirit, but to explain to all of you that **seeing** is not always of importance. The **belief** in messages and the belief in understanding are more prominent in your minds and your makeup. Hold onto the fact that even the slightest visual image can come to you for only a split second. You must absorb this idea. This is what we wish you to look at.

Audient messages may be amongst the most

confusing because they require discipline in understanding the difference between your own thoughts and those of Spirit. Many times over, all of you have heard a word or two, or had an impulse to react to a situation or even speak differently. This was caused by Spirit's intervention. How many times have you been backed into a corner by someone and when you go to defend yourself, regardless of how frightened you may be or nonconfrontational your personality is, the right words seem to flow out of your mouth? You have channeled, or picked up in an audient manner, and verbalized the power that Spirit has to offer you all the time.

Originally, this lesson was not going to even mention the fourth psychic ability, the fourth one being prophetic. However, I thought it would be more approachable if I explain briefly the differences. Understanding Spirit means understanding that we are here only with our highest intentions for your highest purpose in life. Nobody is steered wrong intentionally. Any messages you receive from Spirit are always messages given with the highest probability. We have talked of free will in the past, and it is the will of the human—not necessarily your own, but others—that have impact on you that will greatly alter the spoken words of Spirit. We are discussing this tonight because in the very near future, we will be seeking your interest in understanding the workings of Spirit and other spiritual groups, as well as promoting the concept of a Higher Power through networks. The foundation for this has to be laid now because it is for naught if you do not understand that even those who feel completely shut out psychically are still receiving and answering spiritual messages.

The last great prophet since Christ Jesus was Nostradamus. Ironically, most of his messages came to him while he slept, just as Edgar Casey went into deep trances and appeared to be sleeping. Nostradamus was given information while he relaxed his body, and upon awaking, detailed in his writings what he had seen. There were occasions when he would channel openly to the mass population. His foresight was unacceptable during his time period.

Many messages we give you seem senseless, but take form months or years later. We can discuss your life's direction and pattern for several years to come, but if you sit back and wait for it to come to you, it won't. The power of Spirit works in conjunction with the power of the human being. Hand in hand, each must go. You cannot expect psychic improvement without first trusting yourself and then trusting Spirit. Attempting to look for messages will create a block and nothing will be given. Optimization comes when there is a more carefree, but trusting attitude. This is what happened even with Nostradamus. He did not understand anything at all about the prophecies that he was receiving. He did not know how to properly portray the atomic bomb, yet it was in his writings. His last predictions seem to stem around the close of the last century and the destruction of Earth. While his accuracy may astound people, it must also be noted that a lot of his prophecies have been altered through the power of prayer.

What we have been teaching you is that growing spirituality brings about such an all-inclusive energy exchange of goodwill that the negativity of desecrating the earth becomes something of the past and at the very least, minimized by the combined alliance of prayers. This means that even the strongest, most fear-producing messages can be reshaped by the virtues of peaceful, consistent praying.

We have all been learning together. While it is Spirit who holds the class for all of you, it is all of you who teach the teachers many new things each day. Human reactions, human feelings, and emotions are all given to Spirit and those of the highest plain to incorporate into their future messages back to the people. The Master Jesus was the last pure prophet. What I actually mean by this is that His messages were derived directly from the God energies, and at this point in time, there is no one on the earth's surface receiving the energies directly. This should take quite a bit of pressure off each of you. [Said with humor.]

The powers, or ways, of infusing messages that Spirit brings to you vary greatly. Your spiritual path is not directed by how much you open psychically, but rather by how much you grow as a person. The more you understand this in the physical sense, the higher your soul evolves and the more productive you become. If you understand life in the simplest context, you understand that it is not meant to be that much of a struggle.

If each of you live your lives with contentment, rather than always wanting more, your soul becomes more peaceful and rises higher and faster when the time comes. This does not mean that you should settle just for what you have because the abundance of prosperity, which translates into nice homes, friendship, and love, is always available to everyone. For this, you should always set your goals and work hard to keep them in front of you at all times. Understand the power of all forms of communication that Spirit has to offer you in the form of assistance and your piece of infinite prosperity will be given.

*   *   *   *   *   *

One Feather—I come to all of you with dignity, love, and friendship. When I speak to you, I speak as your brother, perhaps as your father, but always as your friend. I come as a teacher, but I find that it is I who am taught. Even in spirit, understanding spirituality is an ongoing process.

Depression is an earthly emotion, yet in spirit, frustration is evident. Perhaps this frank statement is given so that you feel less belittled or overwhelmed with life. This is often a problem for many of my friends. I share with you that Spirit does not always control your personal situations; however, we send the awareness to nudge you in the right direction. The frustration I mentioned comes because so many humans simply dismiss the impressions they sense and feel. We will keep working with you no matter how long it takes.

I have come mostly to tell you that many people can easily feel my words and stamina-filled energy. It is felt even more readily by the animal kingdom, including cats, dogs, and all of the Great Spirit's wonders that roam in the openness of the universe. They have an inborn

19

knowledge and ability to know when to hunt for food, when to flee for their own safety, and when to befriend anything that will offer simple gifts of goodness to them. It is not complicated for the kingdom of lower souls because they trust in the sensing that radiates throughout their bodies. This is the true compensation and a way to have them safely evolve and survive for millenniums. These brother and sister souls have learned to absorb this protection because, in general, their mental acumen is limited when compared to people. They cannot clutter their impressions with their brain. It all relates to trust.

It is interesting to note that animals have the capability of healing just as humans do. As a human, you have the power of the mind and the ability to feel or accept the energies of Spirit into you and then extend them to others. As an animal, you heal through love, compassion, and the healing energies generated through the mouth. Notice next time when you see a wounded animal and watch as it licks its wound repeatedly, often doing this to their partners or pride mates as well. As you have hands to direct the energies, the animals' only tool is actually the tongue. Regardless, both methods are connections to a higher source of energy.

The most important thing I can tell you is to just trust your inner guidance—that voice within yourself that you feel comes from yourself, but in actuality, comes as a free and willing gift from the powers of the Great Spirit.

*   *   *   *   *   *

Kwan Yin—The message I bring forth is only one of

love, peace, and contentment. I will tell you that my energies are felt differently than the Egyptian's, White Eagle's, One Feather's, Jesus, your family or friends, or anyone else in spirit. It is my intention just to let you know that there are so many subtle differences in the way Spirit revolves and evolves that it is difficult for all of you, as humans, to detect it. This is why you, in a most assured way, must be aware of your knowings, not of your psychic abilities, but simply of what you know from an inner standpoint. Spirit, God, and all those who assist you praise you, bless you, and shed upon you the strength and peace of the Light and the energies of Love that exist throughout the universe.

*   *   *   *   *   *

Sometimes I look at and review the words that were given to me and can easily find ways that they would make better sense. Usually, I tend to leave them as close to what I channeled in because Spirit is always reminding me that what works well for my way of processing things may not work at all for a majority of others. Periodically, you will be reading something that may make virtually no sense to you, but if you ask a few others to interpret the words, a surprising number of different concepts will be given. This is the way Spirit works.

Over the years, I have learned that we are not supposed to have every piece of information at our disposal. There are many times when life is not to be altered so that we can learn and grow from a particular experience, whether it is positive or negative in our view.

The outlook we have isn't necessarily the same approach of the universe that Spirit has. There have been many times when something is said to me that makes me feel so confident that I know exactly what the message is about that I don't even take a second look at it. Ultimately, when the issue plays out in the future, there is generally a twist to what I thought it would be. This keeps me from becoming too satisfied and egotistical in thinking I have everything all figured out.

Spirit will always find ways to reinforce what they want us to know. Sometimes the connection to them is unbelievably canny and comes in incredibly unique ways. It is also a reminder that there are truly no coincidences in life. One day I felt frustrated because of my lack of production and didn't know how to turn it around. After mumbling to myself about what I needed to do and questioning why it didn't happen, I was cleaning up the kitchen table and found a fortune cookie slip that my son must have left. It read, "Affirm it, visualize it, believe it, and it will actualize itself." Once I stopped thinking about why that particular fortune wrapper remained on the table, I understood the reinforcement of Spirit's intent for me, as well as for all of us.

Many times, the messages I channel in from Spirit for the weekly group are well-timed for the majority of whoever happens to be present that night. Personally, I am unaware of it until the end of the proceeding, when several of the participants in attendance come up to me after Spirit's presentation. Most tell me, "I felt like they were talking directly to me!"

I have noticed that as my personal schedule has gotten

busier, that I have lost out on opportunities to channel inspiring messages or words of encouragement that seem to target specific personalities. When I receive them, I usually look at them as a special message. A few of them follow now.

THE CALL TO ARMS

People assume that a call to the spiritual path entails prolific fanfare. The fact is that the opposite is more frequent. Burning bushes, impressive claps of thunder, lightning, and booming voices from the sky and other highlighted calls are merely used to implore the population to always be ready for an astonishing request.

The call to the ministry in many cases is actually just a call to a brighter path—the path that leads you to your higher purpose. How foolish it would be to believe that only revered people are called to service. Perhaps what is trying to be said is that God and Spirit want everyone on the lead row to strive for eternal grace, peace, and protection. Being armed to serve God is being given the acknowledgement that you are a special and beloved child of Spirit. You are asked to produce positive results.

Alone in the battle, you are not. With a penchant for finding leaders who can best administer the teachings of the golden rule and infuse in the physical mind the understanding of Universal Law, God has created an institution where all people are created equal. Only the advanced souls and those who want to obtain a higher and better language of the use of this lifetime are given the opportunity to lead.

As a group, the selection of leadership is such that you are called upon through an inner voice, a nagging feeling. **You are the hope of the future**. Through your work, your interpretations, the earth becomes a place of harmony. Utopia is seen by many as being heaven. The Creator made the universe so that all souls would be a part of this perfect world. Your calling is given to you so that at any time and any place, you may be summoned to step up. Absorb the euphoria in knowing that your ability to lead is being called upon by the simple virtue that you understand and want to improve life. Leadership should be welcomed by the strong. Those who want to find the path should then embrace by following.

The Light upon and within you is the road to recovery. The reformation of your soul is the calling to the Universal Ministry. Absorb, embrace, become one with all.

*   *   *   *   *   *

Time admonishes those who misuse the opportunity to strive towards happiness. God has invoked this as a right of all people. Try not to let the turbulence of life become treacherous to your soul.

*   *   *   *   *   *

**THE EGYPTIAN—
THE ENERGY OF YOU**

As the winds whip through the willows, the voracity of its measure being felt by so much around, a gentleness of Spirit pours through. We are in pursuit of your happiness, the extent of which will never completely be known. In times of turmoil, our silence can be deafening. It is all of the God powers that transcend upon the earth with agility and quiet defiance of any and all misgivings. Imagine **this power you have** and most don't even know it or exercise its use.

As the sun scorches the grains of sand and time, valuable lessons of love and respect are being taught to you as the ornamental environment all people co-exist in and become etched in poetic resurrection. How sweet the heat of Light, the passion of energy that this represents. You symbolize the effort and strife that chasing perfection requires. Spirit assuredly stays in your souls to assist in all that you wish to bake into your earthen bodies.

As the emotion of the raging oceans and seas arrive at the shorelines, confidently and proudly allow the tears of your life to flow with it. Learn that the embodiment of feelings should not be solitary, should not be undefined. It is your life in which it must ebb and flow, like the mightiest of tides. Purification of the soul comes with experience and romancing the inequities that we must all endure. Live within your abilities, your boundaries. Just as the pounding of the water carves its own niche, you have the ability to create the same magnificence with your minds.

As the impression of the moon and the sun illuminate the sky, see yourselves with the fortitude to conquer all.

No challenge is too large, no life around you too small. All are created equal, including you. See this, feel this, and allow yourself to imbibe on the knowledge of vivacity and undying love and support from Spirit and everything it represents. You are the focus of your own creation, your own wind, water, sun, and moon. Like the infinitesimal sand grits, allow life to amass from the wee size of one into the gargantuan ability and love that can be produced.

*   *   *   *   *   *

ANIMAL LOVERS TRIBUTE

One day you came into my life, and I was relieved. I had almost given up on you. Now I knew everything would be all right. I found my friend.

Early in our relationship, I was unsure of myself and so many questions were asked, like: How much could I get away with? Was it okay to taste the food on the counter before everyone ate? Did I really have to use my bathroom, or could one more desirable be appropriate? Could I leave my toys on the floor? Did I really have to eat what was made for me? Would you cuddle with me or just hold me for no reason? Did I have to use the right equipment just for a silly drink of water or was the toilet okay? Could I stay in your room while you had some private time with someone else? Would you hold me in your arms and instinctively know that I needed loving too? When I get sick, would you really take care of me?

26

Would you always love me, no matter what I did?

As time passed, each of these questions received an answer, with the last one getting answered first. And yes, I loved you too. But I knew that when I picked you out to be my family. We've shared a lifetime of happiness together, although maybe not as long as each of us would like. Now, as happens to all good souls, it is my time to move along and get closer to God. I didn't mean for you to feel bad when I became ill. In my mind, helping you was all I really wanted to do. Sometimes, some of my animal friends would share stories with me about their relationship with what they called their Master. I would tell them stories about things that happened between **my friend** and me. They didn't understand.

It is my time to go back to the eternal kingdom, where an animal is safe to be an animal. Do not shed too many tears for me as you helped me to a better place. I am fine. My natural family is here. Some of my friends are here. God is here. My suffering ... well, that's gone. Just remember that my soul will be with you, my memories jam-packed with the great times we shared. Because of your love, your friendship, and your patience, I leave you with an open heart. I'm truly loved in two places. You have given me your blessings at my finest hour. I knew you would when I first met you and for this, I leave you with our fond memories and most of all, I leave you with my love, always your pet.

*   *   *   *   *   *

Dispersed amongst those messages were others. The

following pages were given to me over a couple of days, and although it may seem as though the thoughts and topics meander, it is one of the most comprehensive lessons relayed to me. It does require a deeper thought process and evaluation in order to grasp the gravity of what is being stated. While I make no comparison, it is very much like the teachings that are recorded in the Bible. Some phrases and wisdom translate differently from one person to another. Even through time, the bulk of the message remains steadfast, but the delineation may vary a bit.

THE EGYPTIAN—

CHANGE—This is the ability to accept life the way it was intended to be. Through change and understanding, we, as a mass force, are able to create. We create love, happiness, sadness, anger, laughter, insecurity, confidence, wariness, trust, and so much more.

It is the "trust factor" that might possibly be the most important aspect of all these emotions. By trusting, it enables us to use the senses of our system and the so-called sixth sense as a means in which to communicate what we want out of life. Better stated, it is the capability for which all people can rely on themselves and others to bring about a higher sense of purpose and understanding. We can utilize trust as a cornerstone for success and individuality. We can use it to determine a new path and direction in our life, thereby creating change. Is it then possible that "change" and "trust" are interchangeable?

The answer to that question is a thunderous "NO," because change is inevitable and trust is internally created or substantiated by each individual. Life will always be changing. At no point is it ever without change, whether it is your breathing patterns, exercise patterns, eating habits, or emotional disruptions. These can be for good or bad, depending on how you want to see it. Some people have been embarking on a much stronger spiritual path now than they were a few years ago. This has made for an easier transition into accepting God and Spirit as being routine, rather than just through the edification of religion. The ability to see God in our everyday lives is now more easily seen and done so, without feeling it in an abstract manner, or like you're the exception rather than the rule in society. Years of mainstream religious philosophies have caused a great majority to feel as though the Kingdom of God is something that can only be had in times of dire emergencies or death. The time is ripe for change in all regards. What you do with this newfound knowledge of change is up to you.

Change can be found at the pith of happiness. We laugh because someone has told us a joke that has changed our thought for that moment. We smile because an acquaintance or even a stranger has nodded hello or sent a warm smile your way. The energy around you was shifted because of this, and you embraced it with love. There is always the possibility you felt the love, but couldn't understand why a simple smile would make you so happy. Spirit sees to it that you are always smiled upon.

Through actions, rather than thoughts, you all have the courage rising within your own souls to bring change to the universe and environment. For a moment, I want you to **imagine yourself** as a deer, a bear, a rabbit, or any of God's other wonderful creatures as your home is destroyed. Visualization is a most important aspect of any type of change. You are helpless and at the mercy of man. You have nowhere to turn for assistance because you are not human, but to you, your home is as sacred as any well-constructed frame house or mansion. The trees, meadows, and brooks are as important and secure to you as the roof over your head is to mankind. Animals adapt. They change in order to survive. Spirit cannot understand why the change has to be in learning to cope with less when space and property are abundant.

Now you can return to yourself, to whom you are now. Would you like it if outsiders came and told you that they were taking most of your home? That change most likely would leave you sad or angry. Understanding this, then go and create happiness for the animal and plant kingdom. Find time to donate to help clean up dirty property or find a valuable organization to assist so that you can bring happiness to the lower kingdom. It will also undoubtedly bring peace, happiness, and contentment to your own being. There is always something you can do to help. It doesn't necessarily require a monetary attitude that someone else will take care of things. Change your thinking and you make your own environment a more beautiful place. Isn't the beauty of where you live important too? Spirit is constantly looking for ways to motivate mankind to think about all souls, whether in a human form or not. Everyone can make a tremendous difference within his or her own corner of the world.

If we talk about happiness in a different forum, we may talk about it from the standpoint of romance relationships. Why are so many of us afraid to bring happiness into our lives? Is the fear of change holding you back from igniting the passion of life that is for you to behold? Are you so afraid of the unknown that correcting problems or making changes of a larger magnitude are paralyzing you into non-action? Is **not being happy** the accepted version of what you were programmed to believe growing up because you were taught by misinformed adults? Do generational patterns of thinking have to remain the same, or can you have the courage to make progress by altering your way of thinking? Is the desire to make romantic changes caused by your heart, mind, or society? What if it is something far more powerful, but more difficult to understand? Can your soul demand or create changes for you?

It is possible that a combination of these can contribute to a feeling of instability in even the strongest of unions? The subconscious, and sometimes the more recognized conscious level of thinking, will make us either submit to the whims of change or procrastinate out of a fear of being in an unfamiliar setting. Either way, ultimately you have to move in a forward and more dynamic direction, all the while knowing that God and Spirit are protecting you.

Don't be afraid to engulf modifications in your relationships if happiness has been replaced with complacency, anger, sadness, or fear. This is not an edict to end precious marital vows because Spirit sees and wants long-term contentment in all relationships. The world today makes this a difficult task. Sometimes working at resolving differences with your partner so that you can achieve a permanent, harmonious balance is more rewarding than simply exiting a relationship that feels stale. Not all people can live and accept, without any rancor, the adjustments that their spouses or partners may make while they grow as a person. Relationships are all about changes, both individually and together. The vitality you can feel in working on issues as a unit cannot be easily measured, but it goes without saying that upon conclusion of this segment of your life, you will feel more validated and confident in yourselves.

Let us not forget that sometimes our soul lessons will put people in our lives that are harmful to us. If you find yourself in abusive relationships, there is no reason to stay as long as you understand that through belief in yourself, prayer, and loving family and friends, you can overcome even the toughest of situations. Love and protection from the Highest Power is never absent. It seems that it is always easier for those watching from the outside to recognize the situation of the abused easier than the abused persons themselves. This is why friends and family have an obligation to speak up so that permanent harm will not occur. Make sure you help to make a change that will make a vast difference.

Most people don't realize that change happens the moment we are conceived. We start as two individual pieces of the biological gene pool. From within the marriage of the egg of the female and the sperm of the male, a harmony manifests and life as we know it begins. Like the energy of the spiritual realm and the physical plane, a new balance of power takes shape. This new entity, a person, begins to mature and change, seemingly by the second. Within the normal nine months gestation, an egg and its fertilizer have become a precious little piece of humanity. From the day of physical birth until the day of spiritual birth—or death—as it is known on earth, no one's body goes changeless. This creates opportunity for us. The human body generally gets stronger the more frequently it is used. Exercise is not only good for the physique, but also the mind. If you don't do any, change your philosophy to believing you **can** do it.

Now think about how many times you have changed your mind in your life. Is it wrong to be that unsure or is it proper to always evaluate decisions about things that you may have done differently in the past? We, in spirit, feel it is the best way for you to progress. Use your mind and use it freely. **Take time to break through the barriers of philosophies that have been instilled in you since birth.** Expand the horizons to points unknown and unfathomable in your previous thinking. Free yourself of malevolent musings and offer to yourself the ability to think outside the box. Substantial changes will occur and this will afford you more opportunities to sequester a more positive approach to love and life. There will be many times when you feel like your world is changing in spite of all your best efforts to keep from doing anything different than the normal routine you have worked yourself into. This is commonplace because of Spirit's strong desire to help anyone in need of any type of comfort or change. Use the energy instead of fighting it.

When was the last time you allowed yourself the freedom to stand in the midst of a secluded place and be a child again? Have you overturned rocks to find salamanders? Have you spun until you made yourself dizzy recently? Has the exuberant child within you been free anytime lately? Are you now too old to think you can be impulsive or spontaneous? Is there any joy in your life as simple as when you were a child? Are you afraid to laugh out loud at a silly joke for fear that someone might think you are being foolish? When was the last time you didn't express worries about how you might be perceived in society? How long has it been since you went skinny-dipping or "double-dared" a friend? Most of these questions should not sound childish, but instead, should conjure up some long lost memories of happiness.

People change well ahead of schedule at times. Difficult situations at home or on the job make us jaded to the simplicity of life. Technology has given way to seriousness and negativity, even though it also leads to friendships that would not otherwise have happened. Society, as a whole, has changed and we're responsible for it, both in spirit, as well as in the physical world. Things have changed so rapidly at times that we forget about playing jump rope, jacks, or marbles. Each individual does have the power to recreate the past times of glee, but most are afraid because of the way it will affect those around us. Maturity seems to get in the way of being free and relaxed. Basically, I am telling you to take a walk on the beach, sit in a meadow, or just find a mountaintop and absorb the wondrousness that God has presented to you for your **entire** life—not just the beginning of it. Take part in nature and **become part** of the environment.

Let us briefly consider the children in this world. How different is their life going to be based on all the changes that have evolved? Will they have more to gain from it or fewer benefits because they don't have to be as "hands on" with arithmetic, science, or a host of other things? Will you be available to teach them, as your parents and grandparents did for you? Taking time out to assist a young person reaps rewards untold to you. You can show them so many more things than they would be prone to experiencing simply by opening your heart to them. Wasn't there a special adult in your life when you grew up, whether it was family, friend, or someone as special as a dynamic teacher? Why don't you be that special person and create memories that will long outlast all the changes that a child will see? Let yourself live as free as a child should live. Alter what needs to be altered in order for you to be happy.

Change can be a fabulous thing if you allow it to be. Consider that everything we do imprints our future and the future of many others. So I ask, isn't it more important to understand that it is not how long you live this life, but rather, **how** you live it?

We are being led down a path of least resistance, yet we tend to always shy away from it. Can you break the trend? The answer to that is a most satisfying, "Yes, I can." Now is the time for you to motivate yourself to answer the response. You can do this without fear of failure because Spirit is always at your side. We come in many shapes, sizes, and forms. We may come as a surprise win in the lottery when you determine that it is better to give from the heart rather than out of obligation. Historically, mankind has always found a way to rise to the top of goodness. How many wars were won by the aggressors? Did the regime of Hitler stay atop, or did his legacy become one of loathing, hatred, and the symbol of all things bad or evil? He, in essence, became the flagship for people of all races and religions to vow never to allow such a hideous soul to raise himself up to a position of such power so that men and women would cower in fear again. This is why in today's world, action is being taken in much more strident and forceful ways.

Raising your consciousness can magnetize life's fullest and worthiest accomplishments onto your path much sooner than if you plod through and expect things to remain negative. Also, it is more important for you to justify your actions through the development of not just **thinking** in positive tones, but in **acting** on them. Create your change to bring to you joint happiness. In other words, if you lead the way in making changes, then those around you will benefit from the better energy.

Of course, sometimes we are unprepared for the depth of change that distinguishes life as a humane and peaceful right. Times of destruction through natural disasters are one such thing and accepted more readily by the masses of all people. Acts of destruction at the hands of individuals or groups are different. Sometimes though, when drastic changes scar our world through the actions of senseless attacks on our sanctity of life, the difficult task is in remaining prudent and clear in our thoughts of wanting to be vengeful. You cannot expect that all people are as goodwilled and loving as you want to be yourself, or as you want them to be. Many times it is the free will of people without a good soul that creates havoc. In other words, most of the time it is the sheer mistrust of love and life that allows desensitivity of these procedures to take place. Through all of it, God and Spirit will remain a major force in leading the right measures in regaining the balance of the souls of all mankind towards a higher and better moral direction. He will find a way to rebalance His children and the great creation that is this Earth and universe.

*   *   *   *   *   *

During times of crisis, such as acts of terrorism on innocent people, it is easy for many to be discouraged by what may seem to be God's lack of protection and love. Sometimes it is beyond recognition to most people to comprehend His best efforts. Consider that during times of distress and violent acts on our friends, family, and neighbors of all kinds, that compassion rises to its highest levels. It is possible for patience to elevate itself to the point where someone who would have lost control previously to the heinous acts against humanity and taken a life or maimed someone himself, now finds that the anger that was there is unreasonable in the larger picture. This saves many more people than can be measured by anything in police records or the media. It should be worth noting that rarely, if ever, has a complete eradication of life taken place in any single attack. [Spirit is referring to the massive attacks on the World Trade Center and the Pentagon, where more that ninety-five percent of all who were in the WTC buildings survived and ninety-nine percent survived at the Pentagon.] It is easy for us to state that God has called home His angels. Those who committed the atrocities will not go directly into the Light of heaven that is reserved for all good souls.

When does change get taken over by resolve? The answer to this is at the point you feel so frustrated that you cannot find any other way to accomplish things except to forge ahead. It is this action that will make ordinary people rise up to be heard in times of crisis. Resolve is nothing more than determination to convince yourself that there is no stopping anything that needs to be done because of your utter **need to complete** what needs to be done. This is when you see heroes created in times of distress and disaster. You see them in all walks of life: as policemen, firemen, the military that protects you, but more so, as an individual such as yourself, with no recognition of being anything other than an average person. Consider that you are a piece of God and you should begin to see that being average is a far greater thing than you could have ever imagined. Change made because of resolve is an unbeatable combination.

Often, the masses are moved to action when atrocities take place in their own land. It is very easy for the general population to feel removed from horrid activities when they are across the ocean. When a soul goes bad and attacks in something that may feel like your own backyard, even if it's on the other side of the country, you rally with passion and compassion. The diversity of the human population becomes more noticeable, but also more acceptable in most cases. This blend of mankind is exactly what the United States was founded upon, but more significantly, the universe was also. Why is it that something horrific needs to take place before people unite themselves in a show of solidarity and love? We should all work on this attitude during times of peace and prosperity and not wait until disaster strikes. Change your approach to your neighbors and there will be no need to distrust anyone ever again, regardless of where they come from, because the ties of love will stretch over the countries and waterways. Do you even know your neighbors? If not, go and introduce yourself. Safe havens come when you can discern whom you are living with or near.

Keep in mind that changes that emerge from such disasters frequently lead to better human rights for a single group or multiple groups of people. In this case, the oppression of women in many countries, heretofore ignored, will be a focal point of activity. [An image of Afghanistan and Iraq] Women will find that they are to be seen as equal to men and that their strength as a society will arouse interest in all free societies. The salvation of their physical souls now will create great dissension in the future so that never in the long run will this type of irrational and tyrannical thinking be a feeder to actions in the same manner. These next few years will prove again that when large numbers of people unify for the greater good that it will be answered accordingly. **God blesses all.**

Can anyone assume what's to come of the food chains and energy sources in the world? Many people are doom-and-gloom seekers. For instance, there are those who have a difficult time seeing into the future in any way other than in the negative. This is the type of attitude that Spirit is trying to adjust. We must find a way for all humans to see and bring out the best in themselves and the population the world over. Can you start making more of an effort to view life as an optimistic gift, or are you satisfied with being in a cynical state of mind? If the changes you wish to happen do happen, they will come more swiftly if you participate rather than wait for everyone else to take care of things for you. It is important to be as impassioned about making efforts on your own to bring the zest of life to yourself. **Spirit frequently sees the procrastination of undergoing any type of change in your personal lives as the sole cause of unhappiness**. Why is it so difficult to utilize your abilities to trust in God as your motivational force in improving your current situations? The truth is that if you do not make the necessary adjustments to bad things, you can end up with people of "evil will" ruining even more of this great universe. The world already underwent one siege of dastardly behavior when Hitler tried to create what he viewed as the perfect ethnic being. No uprising against his actions took place for a very long time. Procrastination and disbelief that someone could be this wicked is exactly why so many millions of innocent people were annihilated. Spirit understands the need for justice to be taken and that sometimes it has to be saved through physical abilities in order to secure a future life of infinite sanctuary.

You have the gift of being able to see a new world created. Incredibly heinous acts of anger and terror are what have given this gift to mankind. It will not come easily and it will not come without hardships. Stay focused on the larger, more peacefully balanced global needs, and atrocities will be limited. It is most important for prayer to be a regular part of your daily routine. This will ensure success. Love will be served.

*   *   *   *   *   *

In my mind, anticipation can be life's great equalizer. It can cause actions and inactions, depending on the perspective you create in your minds. Anticipation can lead people to fears, agitation, or depression, but it can also construct euphoric optimism about the pending direction of life. Change becomes what you seek, not always what you think. In other words, your life revolves with the ebb and flow of your emotions and state of mind. This is what causes motion in any human being. "Motion" is just another way of saying that if you learn to react on what you are feeling, the changes in your life will amount to a movement towards what the subconscious, and sometimes the conscious, parts of your brain are creating.

*   *   *   *   *   *

Devotion to God is devotion to life.

Respecting the gift of life is the same as respecting God.

Through a great sense of courage and fairness,
justice becomes the extension of the will of God.

*   *   *   *   *   *

What change can we create in our children? Are we able to influence them to think for themselves in a free and loving way? Is it possible that in order to break old patterns of thinking, we might have to do it through the young ones on earth? Can the imprint of our thoughts be left on a baby forming in the safe haven of its mother's womb? Will this subsequently reap positive rewards for mankind when this same baby is an adult? Likewise, can speaking pessimistically or prejudicially lend the corresponding negativity when older? At what age is it that human beings are most impressionable?

Some of these questions may pique your curiosity, but the answer to them is obvious. Who we are and how we became what we are grows from the home and personal surroundings people are raised in from pre-birth to four years of age. After that, they will be molded more by outside influences that are shaped by friends, schools, and social patterns. The use of the word "pattern" is more important than you could imagine. All people live their lives in a series of patterns. Learning that you can re-create negative past issues and turn them into a massive force of optimistic energy is one of the many keys to living a more pure and happier life. It also brings wonderful things to you and society. Is there a reason to avoid a better way of life? Change can be magnificent.

*   *   *   *   *   *

*Education is the process of understanding
what we don't know.
To deprive yourselves of this is to say
you have no interest in life.
The fact that you are here takes away any
thoughts of dismay,
as well as depression in life and shows
you that the desire to learn
is also the desire to live in a free, loving,
practical, and growing society.*

*   *   *   *   *   *

*The richness of life can be seen through the hearts of
humanity.*

*   *   *   *   *   *

*May the gift of life be yours to harvest and to hold.
Let the love of God ring within your souls and
yourselves.
See the vest of protection that
Spirit always dresses you in.*

*   *   *   *   *   *

Periodically, Spirit will give me short statements that are to serve us as prayers, invocations, and sometimes just as a focused, positive mantra. I've included a few of them for all of you to browse and, hopefully, to use in good ways.

PRAYERS AND INVOCATIONS

May the Kingdom of God protect and serve me/us.
High Spirit,
usher in the bounty of love and prosperity
that was created for
all to be shared. Use Your omnipotence
to inflame actions and
movements that will make me/us useful in
the highest manner.

*   *   *   *   *   *

I/we pray for the forgiveness of all souls
in this great universe.
May the right guidance come to the
hearts and minds of all mankind.
Let the freedom and freshness of God's Light absorb into
our consciousness. Heavenly Spirit, heal me/us so that
I/we can fulfill our greatness. Allow me/us to have the
humility to carry your plan forward.

*   *   *   *   *   *

*Through Your divine guidance, I will be
made strong. May the
power of Spirit lift me to great and unimag
inable heights. I ask
God, Spirit, and the Brotherhood of Light
to allow me to reach my
maximum ability. May God grant me
blessings that weave through
the soul of my being, both on a conscious
and subconscious level.
Allow the protection and peace of Omnipotent
Power to be etched
into me now and for eternity.*

* * * * * *

*God grant me the wisdom to understand
the simplicities of life.
May you give me the answers and
awareness to embrace the
greatness that life has to offer.
Through the guidance of the
White Light, may a symphony of love
be trumpeted into the soul
of my existence. God grant me the
ability to be healed and to
extend the healing to those who need it.*

* * * * * *

*Oh Lord, allow Spirit to douse me with
the purity of white Light.*

*May I have the power to absorb it for the
intended purpose of
accepting the love and healing that I deserve.
By blessing me
with this ability, I will have the strength to
share the message
of the Highest Power with those I know are in need.*

*   *   *   *   *   *

PRAYER FOR SPIRITUAL HEALING

*I ask the great-unseen healing force to remove all
obstructions from my mind and body and to
restore me to perfect health. I ask this in all
sincerity and honesty, and I will do my part to help.
I ask this great-unseen healing force to help
both present and absent ones who are in need of
assistance to restore them to perfect health.
I put my trust in the love and power of God.*

*   *   *   *   *   *

The following prayer was given to me to pass along to
a young woman who was unable to get pregnant for a
long time. It came through as a traditional novena.
Although I have long since lost contact with my client,
the last I heard was that she had three children.

JESUS' BIRTH PRAYER

Oh Divine child, the miracle of life is you.
From the great strength of
Our Father, to the hope of Infinite
Love sent forth to you from the Christ,
remain humble to the tasks of your life
and say the following:

Dear Lord God and all the Teachers of Spirit:
I ask You and the
Benevolent Mother to assist me is reproducing
the Miracle of Life.
I ask this with all my loving energies and
promise to You that I will
persist in the teachings of those in the Light.
I most humbly thank you for Your miracles to
bring me a life. Instill
in me the meaning of new life and I will do my
part to extend this love to
others. I am ever grateful to You for the ability to
breathe life into myself,
and I will always praise and love the Holiest of Spirits
for this joy. I have
confidence in all You do.

Say this prayer five times for four consecutive days,
then say it four times
for five consecutive days, then three times
for three days.

* * * * * *

NEW YEAR PRAYER

*I ask God and Spirit to engulf us with the
prosperity of wealth
in this New Year. Please guide us through
turbulent times, but
freely embrace us with your love, admiration,
and abundance on
all levels of life—spiritually, physically, mentally,
and emotionally.
God, please grant us the happiness that was
created for us in this
year and in all years to come. I respect and serve
You in all ways.*

* * * * * *

There have been times when a large event takes place or is about to take place that Spirit has a way of summoning me to receive a message on the subject. The message following came the night of the terrorist attacks on the World Trade Center and Pentagon. I brought it to my store the next morning to copy it for the prayer and meditation group, not thinking too much about the impact of the words. When my friend and co-worker read it, her immediate reaction was to tell me that I should put it on the counter so people could see it. Up to that point, my spiritual life and my business life really didn't

48

intermingle. I did my best for years to keep what I would jokingly refer to as "my two lives" separate from each other.

After some convincing, I did as she suggested. You must understand that the store itself was not very large and the traffic flow, although steady, was never to the volume I wanted it to be. This didn't prevent over five hundred copies of this being taken by people over the next few days. Some women even cried as they read it. I was amused by the fact that complete strangers and people who were not customers before came in to pick up a copy. Even more to my surprise were some phone calls I received from different folks, thanking me for the words.

This was just another lesson to see how much of an impact the language of Spirit can make on people. Although I knew it was pretty deep in intention, for me personally, the words were fairly normal. Maybe it was because I've become so used to the simplicity and healing aspects of my connection to God and all higher figures.

SPECIAL ENTRY— SEPTEMBER 11, 2001

It is God's greatest gift to bring life to people. By no means is God responsible for the actions of evil that were perpetrated on the world today. America was created to symbolize freedom, unity, and total accessibility to understand the Higher Power, yet it is **understanding** that will take many people a very long time to grasp.

From amongst the piles of rubbish and lifeless bodies that the evils of several selfish men created, people will rise to a greater harmony. Humans will learn not to distrust others so readily, but instead, we will teach and learn from this massive tragedy. All of us, both in the physical, as well as the spiritual, will challenge the foundation of life itself to reignite us to acting in and with love as the focus to humanity. We will amass a great sense of unification and stand tall and proud. By way of proclamation and advancements of maintaining a positive and pure life, the ignorance of these hideous actions will be defeated. Fear has no place in living life, and your God and your inner spirit will prove to be correct in this.

We can be angered and enraged, feel emotionally scarred and hurt, but all energies should be put towards rebuilding our reality of a peace-loving life. Use our focus to help, not hinder, a healing. This is a hard task and well recognized that it may be difficult to achieve, but know this: God and Spirit worked tirelessly in the moments leading to this act of free will to insulate and protect as many as possible. These "miracle" stories will be relayed over the coming days and weeks so that you may zero in on them, rather than the viciousness that was needlessly and hatefully thrown at mankind. America stands for leadership and friendliness, but the United States will need to be just that: **UNITED.** In this time of mourning, you must be a front-runner, not just for your friends and family in this situation, but for the entire world to see. You can set the tone for a new and stronger wave of humanity and be the window for all good souls across the world to see through. This adversity can be the eyepiece of the brilliance of the souls of God, inborn in each and every one of us.

May peace and the Light of God's love be restored to all people, all equally important as His children.

*   *   *   *   *   *

A while after the September 2001 incident, Spirit again spoke about it, but in a far less direct sense. Sometimes, I don't appreciate the message for what it is intended to mean until I've had time to read and digest it a few times. They told me this next segment was key to our future stability as long as we absorbed the words to live by.

*   *   *   *   *   *

As our lives progress, determination of those with a desire to harm freedom and its base fundamentals will ultimately be led to a life of futility, frustration, and incarceration. This is meant not only in the literal sense, but also in the spiritual one. God will not allow for evil deeds to go unpunished or [be] rewarded. Anyone spending their energies on things that are seen in disavowed ways by most people will not be helped to live peacefully. Guilt, as well as fear of retaliatory actions, will leave them wary all the time. Ultimately, they will have a fairly early demise, by physical standards, thus, leaving those of pure and positive natures to be free. Once again, goodness prevails.

It is often that we, in spirit, muse about the workings of the human mind. On the gracious side of God, existing in a panacea of love and mutual respect, it seems unfathomable that the soul that is so pure here can arrive in the physical world and be implanted into a body that carries out "devilish" acts of hatred. What lesson is the soul to learn? Is the lesson for the physical being? Change cures all; however, it is not always simple to override the complexity of lessons in order to restore a better sense of right and wrong. We must encourage and enable those in this type of distress to appreciate goodness, love, and freedom.

ONE FEATHER—

ON COURAGE—What is our explanation of courage? To you, my brothers and sisters, it is the ability to overcome horrendous fears. These fears can be physical, emotional, or in the form of phobias. They can be created out of paranoia of the unknown, sometimes even by acts of war and violence. Courage can be the building blocks, the foundation, and formation of heroes.

We find courage to be a quality that is already instilled in the soul. The Great Spirit made sure you would have the ability to face changes and situations in life that you did not forecast for yourself. Courage simply lets you face up to difficult times and tough circumstances. It can help shape your personality and your ability to communicate and share better ideals with people who might not be of the same mind-set or quality.

Courage can make you prepared for an easier handling of illnesses, the passing of loved ones, career issues, your love life, and much, much more.

For many people in today's misguided world, courage gives you the strength to stand up for your awareness, use, and acceptance of speaking freely about the value of believing and tapping into the Divine Energy. This leads me to wondering why so many good people in the world are afraid to honor and talk about their personal relationship with the Great Spirit, your God. I think that those with the strongest sense of satisfaction and courage should be more vocal about this love. All that would be gained is a further drumbeat of the Highest Power into a mainstream sense of living. In spirit, we see that as something most people should not be ashamed of. With eternal and infinite courage already inside of yourself, you shouldn't have to be reminded to be true to the Energy that has given all beings of life just that—life.

*　　*　　*　　*　　*　　*

During another stretch of time, Spirit seemed intent on trying to relay messages about our responsibility to nature, ourselves, and to our friends and neighbors. Some segments are largely analogous and require some thought. It is Spirit's way of getting us to think more deeply about all of our moves in life, as well as a way to force us to see things on a much more interconnected manner.

ONE FEATHER—

RESPONSIBILITY—This is the cornerstone of action for most mortals. Responsibility is an ingrained sense to accomplish all that needs to be done. It can be in the form of material gains, such as working for a living, or it can also be as deep as sharing respect and a magnitude of compassion towards those who depend on you for emotional stability.

What makes us become responsible citizens is a drive within ourselves, our souls, or centered sense of self-respect and adoration for life itself. Have you ever wondered why you struggle to live and breathe? It is the etched response to yourself, to ensure your own survival in this world. In other words, it is the pressing responsibility to your physical essence to maintain its body for the many soul lessons it needs to learn. Sometimes, it is simply reactive, a part of your subconscious behavior.

Acting responsibly takes great inner strength at times. Sometimes, life hands us opportunities to be happy. While this is great, it is imperative that you do not forget all the reasons and people that allowed for your happiness. The circumstances that led you to the path of enjoyment is also the path that should not be ignored. It is important for the momentum of success to stay firm by retaining all the responsibilities that were already in place.

Does your newfound happiness make you stray away from your duties to your family? What about to your job or friends? Do you now forget to feed your pets or offer assistance to all the people who had been relying on you to this point, or do you become too selfish by focusing on just what makes you smile in the immediate moment? Has time management become difficult or simply ignored?

All of these issues are outcomes of responsibility. What you choose to do with yourself, your options, is what will make the biggest difference on your long-term path to success and happiness. It also will mark the success and happiness of all the people you come in contact with in your everyday life. Perhaps what we are trying to get you to think about is the connection between managing your approach to life as a direct outcrop of handling life responsibly.

There is always a direct connection between your own actions and the effect they have on many other people attached to you, both directly and indirectly. Take a moment to think and imagine what would happen to a small town if their main market were forced to close. It is not just the impact on the storeowners themselves, but also all the adjustments that the rest of the community must endure.

One store closing its doors may impact the others by the loss of people traffic. Human nature is traditionally, and always will be, curious at all times. Consider that when we go shopping, we frequently look at all the signs in the windows, even when we have no intention of going in. The draw and curiosity of the human mind and soul is also to always explore. Therefore, natural tendencies have us visit or enter places we may not have intended to go to before.

Now think about the fact that a place of business may draw two hundred people a day. Automatically, all of these people have had their lives affected by the actions of one. They have to find a new routine, a path for themselves that forces change on them, and no matter how small that may seem, all of these people are going to disperse and deal with new faces. This may be good or bad, depending on the attitudes attached. Envision the spiraling effect. What is most important here is not the economic impact on the many, but the fact that their lives were altered by someone they probably didn't even know. With that in mind, are you acting in a responsible way? Can you wake up each day and know you did your best not to negatively create a steamroll of ill-advised issues for yourself or the dozens of people that could be connected to each decision?

Let us look at this from a personal standpoint. What if you were feeling severe aches and pains that you never had before? Would you go and get checked out by the medical community, or would you risk something more serious? The answer to this question is vast. Any action you take, whether it is immediate and firm, or weak and indecisive, will have repercussions on your family and friends. The decision will have an affect on the life of doctors, nurses, and others. If you are thinking that the only way you change someone else's life is by taking action, guess again. By not acting on certain issues, you put yourself at risk, the value of the doctor at risk, and your family is in danger of losing someone close to them. All of these examples are not being given to make you paranoid about what you should do, but to get you to see how even the simplest of things can change the vibration of so many others.

The world revolves in an interconnected way at all times. Nature, be it the plant or animal kingdoms, has been left to human society to watch over and protect its creations. To this point, we have done a poor job. In a society that focuses on material gains, regardless of how environmentally sensitive you may think you are, abuses still occur. This is part of an accepted master plan, but it is equally imperative that you do everything under your power to recycle whatever is possible. This will align you with one of the Laws of the Universe. If left undisturbed, all of life and its natural items return to the bosom of Mother Earth. Each aspect feeds off the other, but by changing the balance of nature, disruptions and frequent deaths take place. This is just another reason to act in a responsible manner.

Sometimes responsibility stems from dedication to oneself. If there is an internal call or yearn to finish, comply, or accomplish that which you set out to follow, then approaching life responsibly is the fastest way to achieve it. There will be many times when the knowledge of why you feel pulled in a certain direction will be unknown to you. Let this not be a problem since the soul oftentimes is responding to a higher call.

Consider that we truly do choose the life we come into. Perhaps then, your reason to be responsible is skewed by the desire of your child, spouse, or other relation. It is more than possible that their life is the driving force in keeping your own path honed towards and for the right causes. To keep this simple, where would any child be if there were no responsible adults to feed and care for them in the beginning stages of life?

Under the same premise, where would your soul be if you did not nourish it and treat it responsibly? You have the control to take it and use it for all of its highest good. Remember, you are the keeper of your soul. This means that you owe it to yourself and to God and the Higher Powers to be the best person you can possibly be. Striving for success and goodness is an honor bestowed upon you by the Great Spirit. This is all the more reason that you have to trust and follow through with any and all requests of Spirit.

If you feel you can control your silence to feel the voice and child within yourself, you are able to understand what Spirit wants of you. Sometimes, the messages will oppose what you feel or think you need in your own life. It is exactly this point that makes following and trusting your God and Higher Power seem to be an impossibility at times. This concept remains one in which even I, One Feather, am working and striving to revive within my soul and your souls too. As your teacher, guide, and brother, it is my mission to offer admonitions when I feel you, the caretaker of a great soul, need to be realigned.

As an incarnated soul, I would practice the art of being naked before the Great Spirit. It was my way of showing Him that I had complete love and trust in Him. As strange as this might seem, it empowered me. I did not do this to disrespect any of my friends and neighbors, but to show the Highest One that I truly did have faith in Him and all of the nuances of the messages sent forth to me. As a leader, I was respected by many in my community. They, however, did not know of the stresses I felt in trying to answer to my God and higher self. It frightened me, even back then, to be made to feel so vulnerable, yet at the same time, an infusion of power would come over me when I willingly gave myself up to the Spirit I followed.

In today's time, it would be much more difficult to respond to this same task, as there are very few private places and open land areas that would enable the same empowerment. Respect of everyone, especially the children, is always primary. Respect of God is also necessary. How do we balance the need to administer Spirit's wishes with the reality of the physical world? The simple answer is that we trust in ourselves. We must trust in ourselves as individuals and as a larger part of society and the world around us.

Being true to your soul and your God is what responsibility is all about. What about the symbolism of what I speak? Did you ever take time to see how free and easy the kingdom of animals live? For a moment, I want each of you to think about the responsibilities that all living creatures stand up to. The eagle is a strong symbol of courage and freedom. It soars high above all else and scans the land for potential prey and nourishment. The eagle fills itself with respect, dignity, and desire to survive. Are you a survivor?

At the same time, the kingdom of animals understands its place in the cycle of life. Predatory animals are sustained by controlling the populations of smaller ones. The smaller animals survive by eating insects and the like. The insects pollinate the plant kingdom, while at the same time they nourish themselves. When the season ends, the plants wither and meld into the ground, thereby creating natural nourishment for the soil so that everything can repeat. This is admittedly a very simple way of looking at life, but when one aspect of the natural chain is disturbed, the balance of life up and down the links of life is disrupted. Since we, as humans, are the highest in this command, it is our responsibility to nurture and not destroy the perfect balance that was created for us. What do you do to maintain your positive part in this evolution? Do you abuse the resources created or do you reasonably and responsibly do your absolute best to regenerate in proper ways by reusing or recycling?

*   *   *   *   *   *

Allow the fires of the soul to burn free and bright.

*   *   *   *   *   *

A path of recognition only becomes so when we learn to venture towards the unfamiliar.

*   *   *   *   *   *

CEBALOS—

The thoughts of my wisdom and instincts include righteousness in believing we are all indicators of free will and a free world. Our responsibilities lie within the makeup of our personal constitution. Who we are and who or what we want to leave behind as our memory, or legacy to life, is tantamount to what we want to be remembered for.

Is there ever a time in which you wanted to take back negative thoughts or statements to others that bordered on the malevolence of our anger? How many times have you reviewed the verbiage you spewed before thinking? How many times have you done this just in catching thoughts within your mind? The wickedness of our minds can directly produce the outcome of events in our futures. This is precisely why I have been fervently working on passing along the edge of kindness and kind acts that all souls need to have in order to be nourished and guilt-free. It is the responsibility of the guardian of the soul to produce this. You are the guardian.

There are times when we see the physical world as a place of complacency and decency. Then, there are the times when we see it as a place of contempt and indecency. We must all find a way to diminish anger and to increase tolerance. The world runs more smoothly when this simple, yet difficult to achieve concept is administered in the most pious of ways. Keeping life simple is not as much of a chore as many people want it to seem. The philosophy of "letting go and letting God" handle the adversity that beseeches you is the truest and most divine intervention that there is. Allow yourselves to be responsible enough to try this method of dealing with difficult people and all of the situations that are incurred because of them.

We must learn to challenge ourselves into allowing for the differences in others to be acceptable. The free form and flow of love and life comes when we learn not to be judicious in the way we filter everybody else's thoughts and actions. It is our responsibility to allow for the divinity of God's love to exchange the needed thoughts to keep His creation a safe and joyous place to live. After all, isn't this what we are striving for? Isn't it the right of all good people to feel the same sense of security that we felt in the womb of our mothers, in the womb of our Christ Being?

Now is the time for all of us to accept the responsibility that is ours when Spirit finds a way to introduce the people into our life that will help make a difference to us. The odd thing about this is that most of the time we don't necessarily know that this is their purpose. We tend to panic about anyone or anything we are unfamiliar with. Giving ourselves the chance to be on an escalating path of positivism requires us to step into a territory that may be uncomfortable. It is, however, our duty to accept the agenda that Spirit puts out for us. It is our responsibility to embrace newness and creative ways to expand our horizons.

This should be done by asking numerous questions. The first questions you should ask are, "Am I important to so and so?" "Am I important to myself?" **Define yourself**. What is your value? Are you just putting your time in on earth until you are returned to the side of Spirit, or will you try to make a difference? Do you see life as an anomaly, or do you choose to embrace it for the excellence it, and you, can create it to be, or even become? Is it an inconvenience, or do you want to excel to raise the vibration and aura of your soul?

We feel life is magnificent. The Creator made this universe for an untold, and perhaps, infinite, number of lessons. By understanding this, you become entrenched with the belief and necessary discipline to abscond with as many vital and rich attributes that are available. In other words, you have to live up to your responsibility to yourself, your soul. You create a more dynamic and uplifting energy for others to see and use.

When we are born, it is purity of the soul that reigns, but it is the parental guidance that first dictates our direction. While this is necessary, it is also the leading cause of delays in long-term happiness. We are a product of our environment. Frequently, when our life has trouble shifting forward, it is not always our own fault. Physical beings all wallow through the insecurities and energy drains or fulfillment of life as seen by our guardians. This does not always make for a perfect harmony. Through the embracing of your own soul's direction, the ability for you to vibrate to a more potent energy and person is, and will always lie, within the responsibility of oneself. If you can understand this concept, you will then be able to make more headway towards a prosperous life.

To more concisely explain this, it would be to say that all people are working within the energy fields of others. As this is true, then it stands to reason that if you are brought up in a household that contains negativity by a guiding figure, then you and your soul have to fight that much harder to be the counterbalance and imbue a positive approach to life. This is why it is so vital for you to represent to all young people that behavior that envelops love and respect will impact the future of the world in ways more responsibly and optimistically. It becomes a direct link to world peace and at the very least, tolerance of others.

By being able to do this, the human mind will open to greater capacities. You will not feel ridiculed for thinking outside the normal parameters of what you were taught. Instead, you will be a paragon for pure beliefs and adventure. Through an adventurous attitude, the desire to ease and erase all illnesses and social disorders becomes second nature. Working within the energy fields of others is tricky at best. It requires the transmission of a pure and divine thinking, of a relentless connection to one's higher self. The attributes of individual souls are such that they are predisposed to wanting to please and be recognized as a good entity for all other people to infuse into their own field of spiritual energy.

If this is true, then so is the opposite. There are those people who chronically feel the need to be superior, thereby creating a wave of insecurity in many people that are in their energy field. It is these people who actually feed off the goodness of a more positive person, although it is done without them being aware. They are absorbing the essence of your goodness just so they can survive in a world of beautiful energies. Their insecurities in life actually cause them to reach out towards the type of person they aren't. If this sounds a little confusing, it is only because you are already in the mode of being a better human, simply because you are taking the time to improve your universal thoughts of life. It is commonplace for you, but not for the ones of negative ilk. You are continuing to amass an etched soul memory of purity.

Sometimes our words to you are designed to force you to think. If you learn to internalize Spirit's rationale, then you are on the road towards entitlement and preservation. We don't always look for things to confuse the population, but we do look to press a deeper sense of awareness that everything you do is for the betterment of life as a whole.

*   *   *   *   *   *

The Light within the child is bright enough to lead the way for the future of all adults. All of mankind can be this child. A wave of humanity will then sweep across the globe. The creation of kindness and tolerance then grips the hearts and souls of all on earth.

*   *   *   *   *   *

Virtuous living is the indicator of a knowledgeable soul.

*   *   *   *   *   *

ONE FEATHER—
DEFENSIVE LIVING

It briefly came to mind that most of us have lived our

lives defensively. For the average person, time and effort is spent in fears and worries about what could be. Instead, allow yourself time to live and breathe with confidence about what might be to come.

In my mind, emphasis on the negative is always more prevalent then emphasizing the positive. It is surely a tough thing to do when we have been programmed to think with caution all the time. Am I asking you to be careless? Absolutely not! However, I am asking for all of you to let go of the defensive posture and absorb living life in a fanciful and more optimistically offensive way— offensive, as in take charge. Let us break down the barriers of happiness. Don't allow yourself to assume that everyone around you is suspicious and automatically up to no good.

When I was incarnate, I lived through an era that was mostly free of the fear of being overrun by ill-willed people. Occasionally, we would have to endure an outburst of savagery by a band of folks that were not tuned into the energy of the Great Spirit. Back then, we didn't need to worry about nuclear weapons or any other mass-produced evil appendages. All that was of concern to us were handcrafted arrows with an array of poisonous herbs added to the tips. Sometimes, flaming projectiles were used as well. Hand-to-hand combat would take place, and we needed to be cautious of sharpened shell or stone knives and whittled branches.

My point is that it was unnecessary for the population as a whole to fear living freely and worshiping in the way we wanted. We honored and respected those who were the elders. Today, society seems to have fears of warlike events that include a barrage of weaponry that was not thought of in my time. People have to fear getting on buses, trains, and planes, which, incidentally, we didn't have either. The world has become full of a defensive people and, therefore, creates an air of distrust and non-tolerance with anyone who differs in color or creed from you. While this is an admitted oversimplification, the truth of the matter is that this is what has led to parents and guardians instilling fear into us from the time we are born. It is a hard way to live.

From the time language is understood, commands are being given to err against the side of safety. In truthfulness, this is not necessarily the wrong education, however, there has to be a limit to how many issues are thought of in negative ways. The eventual outcome is of many humans behaving and living in an aura of paranoia instead of peace and tranquility. For myself, I wanted the energy field around me to be one in which people did not have to feel defensive, but could embrace the love, patience, and trust I wanted to emanate. It was important to me to feel enriched and even more so, for me to make other people feel that way also.

The way you feel about yourself and what matters to you will directly enhance the forecast of your future. Be an example to others and limit thoughts of unnecessary fears. Use the ingrained part of your essence—your soul—and trust that your Great Spirit is available to protect you. This is not naïve thinking. The advice is sound, and if enough people have the courage to turn the tide of dissension, life then can return to the simpler days of yesteryear. I am not abdicating that you throw safety to the winds of the Gods, but I am telling you that you need to begin to evaluate your thoughts about people from dawn to dusk. The reality is that society, as a mass unit, is not going to be of harm to you. However, the evil that resides in the hearts of certain men and women need to be a concern, **but not the controlling factor** that runs your life's actions.

There is a completely different aspect of defensive living. My request is for you to be defensive of the environment, which is clearly your external home. As I review the attitudes of most people, I am alarmed by the fact that many do not see the need to pitch in to help maintain and cleanse the outdoors and all of earth's products, as though it is everyone else's responsibility. The majority of you would be sensitive, annoyed, and defensive if strangers walked through your home dropping cigarette butts, soda and beer cans, candy wrappers, and things like that onto your bed, floors, and food. Think about that. You have the voice and skills to say "no" when something or someone is taking advantage of your residence. The plant and animal kingdom cannot do this; hence, they need ambassadors and loving attitudes to maintain and respect the environment for them.

We would not be able to survive if it weren't for all things that originate from the earth. It is the only basis for our food, medicine, and sustenance to breathe. Why wouldn't you defend it? All of us want to successfully and peacefully enjoy the abundance that God created for us. As a single individual, making changes in your lackadaisical approach towards the importance of reforming your personal behavior and decisions to assist in cleaning, reusing, or recycling what is viable will make for a healthier globe. Do yourself a favor and defend the environment and don't wait for "the other guy" to do it.

In life, there are leaders and those who wish to follow them. There is another, mostly unspoken group of people who want to lead but are afraid of the responsibilities and attacks from the less informed that make it hard for them to act on it. We, in spirit, see leadership as a more personal accomplishment. It can be done from the very depths of your own home and property. How much effort is really needed for you to rinse an empty jar or bottle and place it in the appropriate container to have it recycled? How hard is it for most people to bend over and pick up a piece of wayward trash, rather than wait for this refuse to blow by your property with the hopes that someone else will gather it up? Usually, it is as simple as altering your way of thinking that will encourage you to defend the kingdoms of plants and animals. It's easy. You can all do it.

*   *   *   *   *   *

Allowing yourself to freely love requires you to freely love yourself first. Ignite the Light!

*   *   *   *   *   *

Like the free bird that soars high, love can bring you to unfathomable heights. Make your soul fly high!

*   *   *   *   *   *

My continued lessons are not always given to me as clearly as I'd like them to be. The next few messages started off strongly by One Feather, but as sometimes happens to me, other spirits started voicing their thoughts. At times, I am not fully aware of the shift in energies since they seem to morph from one to another. The only way I can tell is because the cadence of the words seems to be different. My apologies to all of you if this next span of messages seems to jump from one issue to another, but in the end, a lot of information will have been touched upon.

*   *   *   *   *   *

ONE FEATHER AND OTHERS
MIND POWER

It came to my mind today that the good in life can be easily given by the **good in one's own mind.** Have you ever wondered why your life may seem destined to wallow in the same old circular motion while other people are having the time of their life? I was one who thought that way when I was a young lad.

What I soon came to understand was that my misgivings and misfortunes had to do more with my inability to look forward and turn life's opportunities to my advantage. Most people tend to look the other way when the Great Spirit places a chance for change on their path. Change is not something that the ordinary human wants for himself or herself. Let's face it, change is a scary concept if you have no faith in the Higher Self that resides within. But from now forward, I can share with you a better approach.

In order to live life to its maximum capacity, you must first be able to interpret the body, mind, emotional, and spiritual connections. All of these assets are manipulated through thought impulses. Everything in the universe is, in essence, universal in that it is mind flow, ebbing in and away, that eventually leads to the creation of what we have manifested. This is a topic that should be expanded on in the future. The importance of this manifestation is that it enables you, as an individual, to have as much power and potential positive performance as you desire. Why wouldn't you desire the maximum?

The answer to that question is simple and relevant to your education as a growing being. No matter how old, how young, how active, or how assertive, we are creatures of ingrained thoughts and ideas. We live our lives with an etched impression of what is right and wrong for whom we are. The etching comes from what we learn as children from our parents, family, friends, and environment. Sometimes, the greatest influence is not what we conceived after our birth, but what notions were given to us during conception and growth in the safety of the womb. If that sounds startling, consider that our soul is in the learning process before and after the act of physicality takes place. It is an energy with a mission to learn; therefore, it absorbs common thinking even before it finds its home in your physical frame. You are the keeper of an esoteric mass of purity that needs to find answers on a deeper level then could ever be understood by the average person.

What if you are saddled with an imperfect health picture? As a generality, most people tend to think they have no recourse in becoming stronger again. This is an untrue philosophy. You see, the mind is a far more formidable tool than anything that the medical community has invented. In fact, God has given all of you everything you need to become more of a success. You already have an impressive instrument. It is the power of positive thinking, or in other words, the power of your mind.

It has been my understanding that the usefulness set within yourself is mishandled on a regular basis. Most people look past the value of optimizing their mind-body connection. Redeeming the gift the Great Spirit has obliged you with can reverse some illnesses. It is not my want to completely expand on this topic at the moment because the importance is simply that you must **trust** the virtues of what you have available.

The first step in this process, however, is to learn to relate to your inner self, the proverbial "child within" that is so frequently spoken of in society. This inner existence in reality is just your soul. It is an understatement to refer to it as "just your soul," because that sounds like a minimalist approach. The soul is contained within the physical shell of yourself, but it threads through the mind with an energy that can truly rule all aspects of who you are—that being the accepted body, mind, and soul connection. That said, why wouldn't you be able to visit deeper into your consciousness and "rewire" the cells that hold you together into something more harmonious? What I am saying here is that you can rebuild your molecular structure to be hardened into a positive structure, one without obstructions, by simply using the visualization approach.

You can, and will, be able to see yourself in a place of safety by quelling the external noise near you and actually allowing yourself to feel the harmony and gentleness that is capable of being grasped. It requires discipline. Because of normal physical occurrences, distractions are routine to quietness. This is why it becomes imperative for you to limit to the greatest degree, any and all disruptions within your personal control. Only then will you be able to advance your mind towards the tranquility of your soul.

Once this is accomplished, the pleasure of serving yourself better because of the capability to brighten yourself through the power of positive mind control will lead you to a new awareness. It is an awakening of something that has always been available to you since birth. Now that we have simplified it, what are you going to do? Will it be life as usual, or will you foster new beginnings and steer your path towards one that is stocked full of achievements waiting to happen? **Now** is always the time to begin.

With this "old" information clarified, you can now undergo various ways to express the art of visualization. The mind and the imagination are boundless, not confined to a physical presence. That has to be thought about and understood. How far outside your usual frame of mind can you take yourself? Can you envision yourself simply in a nine to five job, running errands, walking the dog, or are you able to see yourself someplace more rewarding? If you try, can you see yourself caressed by a gentle breeze, a mist of warm, sea or fresh water moistening your face, the warmth of the sun glistening on your cheeks?

The option you choose can directly lead to a stronger frame of mind and a healthier body. In order to use the magnificence of the mind to heal, you need to be able to purify the "place" you see it in. The more harmonious and happy you can envision yourself to be, the more easily the physical body takes shape to fit that description as well. This includes balance in personal relationships and all pertinent aspects of your life. The judgments and emphasis you place on each issue tends to directly lead to the speed in which physical recovery is possible. I cannot tell you that all illnesses can be cured, because there is the always-present aspect of life lessons or soul lessons that need to be answered.

Some of you may have had to endure unfair situations in your journey through the world. Even the most ostensibly erratic and annoying problem can be alleviated through mind and body alteration via the use of visualization. That might seem a lot to comprehend, but the simplicity returns to the fact that all you need to do is trust the power of your mind. Are you able to see a small flame that flickers at first, but then turns into a roaring blaze? If so, you have just envisioned the power and way the mind links to its surroundings. Just like a flame as small as from a match, fanning it with oxygen makes it grow. Your ability to evolve your thinking to reach outside the parameters that were given to you by others is quite truly the same as the oxygen. It allows you to perform magnificent things from small beginnings. Life is like this all the time.

For those of you who are dealing with an illness, my question to you is, "Do you see yourself in the peak of fitness, or do you see yourself as already beaten?" This is an important question. Most people tend to look at themselves as being on the downside of things when an illness or physical mishap besieges them. How different would your outlook be if your attitude allowed you to take on the negativity face-to-face? It bears repeating that negativity moves at a slower vibration than optimism and being positive. This simply means that if you can exhort yourself to maintain a balance and protection against the negative, then you have automatically given yourself a gift of improved potential for any and all healings you want, whether it is physical, emotional, or mental.

For a moment, I want to stress to you the valiance in mentally, or "mindfully," growing spiritually. There is a vast difference in outcomes in life if you trust the Great Spirit, the Higher Power around you, and to a great extent, the power within yourself. This simply means that you are aware and accepting of an energy that can be tapped into for the promotion of all good things. Don't ever be afraid or feel unworthy of talking to Spirit. Some of you have been raised to think that praying is only useful in a format that was church-authorized, yet in spirit, we find that words from the heart are more relevant. This is because you are, in essence, letting all of us on the side of Spirit know that you are a warm and wanting person.

There is, however, a difference in being a wanting person as opposed to a person who is simply working their way through life as a needy one. You see, we look at those who have not learned to open up to the great realms of possibility as the same ones who need to be targeted for mind-altering messages from beyond, at least from beyond the physical world. In order to do this, those who come across as needy must begin to see their own potential first. If they can do this, then the need to be needy is removed and they become more prosperous and helpful to society, rather than wait for society to come to help them.

There is a huge difference between acting needy and truly being this way. Spirit sees those who rely on others without making an effort for themselves as not being deserving of the strength of gifts from the world. In order to succeed in life, you must have the foresight and forethought to make it happen. This is a true statement, whether it is for general financial gains or what we are discussing here, which is the health of the human body. Once again, the power of the mind is the greatest tool you can have to improve anything.

I have told all of you that the skill of visualization can turn out to be the key to the mastery of life. Locked away for most of you is an art form of joys and happiness. It is your safe haven, a place where you can take yourself to rid the stresses of everyday living. It is a healing and uplifting energy and can enable you to amount to become anything or anyone you want to be. Hesitation in doing this only delays the better outcomes that are available to you. Why not let your mind show you precious images of happiness and good health? Arc you afraid to uncrate the dilemmas caused by infused thought patterns given to you by others? Be free! Be brave! Be bold!

This has been told to you because I am using **my** mind power to generate actions on your part, just for simply reading or hearing these words. Your reactions create the avalanche of necessary movements within your heads. Obey these next words as I am able to see for you the heaviness of your illnesses lifting far away from your physical body. The darkness of your maladies is being transformed into a shelled light and sent to a safe place on the side of Spirit, a place that will help enable you to stay healthy and strong. In my mind, I am seeing a swirling light heading towards each affected area, and then encasing it with a magical sparkle. It rises out of you and hurtles towards space.

That was perhaps one of the simplest visuals you can do for yourself. If anyone complains that they can't do that, then I tell you that you are not putting out any effort at all to fix your body. Perhaps for you, it is the intelligence that needs to be looked at. This is not to say that any of you are stupid, but instead, to let you know that you must learn to unlock the density of preconceived notions. In other words, you have to let go of what you know and feel is comfortable.

Understand that many of the mainstream religions frown upon holistic healers because they don't line up with their teachings. Yet, it is the same sects that will embrace and advertise for their own gains when they have a religious healer who is part of the ministry. God does not select by title who can or cannot do this type of work. All are capable and embraced by the Great Spirit for their personal abilities to entice healings through just what I have been teaching you. It is through the concept of mental pictures and absorption of the Light—Energy—that makes healing possible. Mind healing is not abstract, not voodoo, not evil, and not improper. It is simply the use of clearing out the negative in the physical body through the succulent use of the natural energies that God and Spirit have given you.

Another direction you can take mind power to is to use it in pain management. This may be one of the easier uses as it is simply put to work by understanding that the physical body is far more resilient and resistant to pain than most people think. There are some who get panicky and pass out at the sight of a needle or cry mercilessly if they get pricked by a pin. I have found that most pain is a reaction to an event, and not always relevant to the actual physical discomfort. It is the real pain that I want to invite you to look at.

One of the easiest ways to reduce discomfort is to learn to take advantage of deep-seated breath work. Just as when you are told to take a big gulp of air and count to ten when you are angry, the same general philosophy holds true for pain management. Don't disagree with this theory before trying it because it is as simple as I have just stated. It is not anything more than a way for you to be in control of what you are feeling before letting the imbedded fears and feelings dictate to your brain that it is supposed to feel pain. If you take control, then the pain can't. How simple is that?

The more acceptable and long-term way to limit your pain is through a steady regimen of meditation. On many levels, meditation can put the body into a transitional state of relaxation and contemplation. I use the word "contemplation" as a suggestion that you can take the physical body wherever you want. In other words, you have the choice to leave it feeling ravaged without a fight, or you can meditate yourself into a zone of safe havens and stress-free situations. You take control of the illness and the illness then does not easily take hold of you.

One form of relaxation through meditation is actually through soft tissue massage. Manipulating the skin can create a soothing chemical feeling within the brain and nervous system. This, in turn, is relayed to the neurological aspects of your body, thereby allowing the system to fend off aggravating aches. Maybe it is just the fact that you allow yourself to be pampered that releases the negatives within yourself. These feelings of negativity are both on a physical and emotional level.

In order for any form of healing meditation to work to its fullest potential, you need to learn to take yourself to a safe time in your life. Go into the meditation with the awareness of some of your happier memories. This enables you to review what it is like to be without problems, illnesses, and substantial pain. Perhaps it can be seen as the new age of pain management. Make sure, my brothers and sisters, that you have some fun with where you take yourself. Keep in mind that no two people have absolutely identical havens of safety, so concentrate on yours only and filter out the input of what other people tell you is your place to be.

For some, it may be that you are nestled in the bosom of your mother as a small child. Others may see it as a time in their childhood when playing with friends on a playground or in the dankness of someone's basement as being sufficient. Yet for others, it could be the glee you felt during a particular vacation or the moment of realization that you knew you fell in love for the first time. Love is probably the greatest healing energy of all.

People tend to think that by using their imagination they are doing something foolish. There is nothing that can be further from the truth. Entwined with your mind is your ability to see what isn't immediately in front of you through the art of imagination. Again, it returns back to mind power. This power is a unique gift given to all people by the hand of the Great Spirit. Use it or lose it! What that means is that if you want to empower yourself, the availability of the power has to be tapped into. It you don't care or don't want to do anything to improve yourself physically, mentally, and spiritually, then let your mind stay dormant. The results will match.

For a moment, I wish to discuss different visualizations to help reduce cancerous growths. The first one for you to attempt is simple, yet more powerful than you could normally hope to believe. With your eyes gently closed, visualize a candle in your mind's eye. Focus on the flicker of the gentle flame. See the color turn from orange to purple, or blue, if that's easier. Now, follow the black discharged smoke as it elevates up and away from the flame. It is important that the next step is imaginative, as I want you to view the smoke rising through and then away from your body. Let it flow through all the points of discomfort and flow out of the top of your head. If you want to, see it coming out of your fingertips or feet, as that is okay too. You are allowing the negativity to go up and out to the realm of Spirit. The continued key is to do what makes you comfortable, and remember that no two people are completely alike.

The second visual for you to work on is also simple and fun. Be creative. See any tumors or growths being prepared for explosion. In your mind, recall images of large buildings being safely detonated, then slowly change the look of buildings into the image you have of the growths. Have fun while you envision them blowing up or being pulverized. What happens when you do this is that you send a signal to your mind that the alien agents in your body don't actually belong there, and more importantly, **they don't belong to you.**

Lastly, I want you to learn to vividly use any method that may be humorous to you that shows anything being dismantled, blown up, or vaporized. Even adults can have fun seeing this in cartoon form in their minds. The use of cartoon imagery is important because it allows you to see yourself in a more energized and revitalized way— perhaps as a carefree child again.

You can consciously retrain your brain to make it clear that you do not want or own the negativity that has invaded you. Make sure that when someone speaks to you or when you are talking about the illness that you never personalize the disease. In other words, it is vital for you to speak of "the" tumor and not "my" tumor. Likewise, when someone asks you how your cancer is, politely correct them into understanding that you do not own it and don't want to own it. These simple philosophies and steps will create an aura of healing. And isn't recovering exactly what you want for yourself?

All of what I have just shared with you stems from the gift of positive and creative mind thinking. It is a significant symbol for you to hang onto in order for long-term and permanent healing to be received. As humans, the hardest thing to overcome is to reverse or alleviate yourselves from previous conceptions of how life works that were given to you from some outside influence, be it family, friends, or something shown on the media. Remember, you are in control! You can take control!

There is never a time in life when nothing can be accomplished if you gain self-control. Within the walls of your body, persistence in the power over all outside influences allows you to dictate what and where you want life to proceed to. Remember the words, "No fear." If you can overcome any and all fears, you set your path towards the optimism and fulfillment that is always desired. The best way to rescind the issues of being afraid is to "under complicate" the issue at hand. I have intentionally used the singular tense because most people have more than one thing that gives them some fear, yet there is a value in not lumping them together. Tackling one issue at a time is sufficient and within that one issue, there usually are some forms of sublevels that can be dissected.

Use your mind to analyze what segments can be separated. In other words, if you have a fear of heights, don't begin looking at tall buildings like the Sears Tower as one unit, but instead, as many, many individual goals to conquer. It would be easy for you to walk through the doors on the ground floor, but not necessarily to the one hundred-tenth floor. Let your mind create a feeling of solidity as you take each step up. This sounds like an easy process, and, in fact, it is as simple as I state it. For those of you who truly are afraid of heights, it is just the opposite, but with practice, it simplifies.

Instead of letting yourself hyperventilate over the mere thought of the building top, consciously begin to place a more optimistic thought of what you have already accomplished. In other words, you need to realize that you have already been to higher places and handily survived. If you lived or passed through the great land of Denver, you were about a mile higher than you would be at the top of the tallest building. Most likely, you didn't take the time to think about it though.

Life is all about molding and twisting confidence through manipulation of what you already know. Since that is the case, make sure you practice. You can do it no matter what the situation, no matter how dire you may deem things to be. Illnesses, fears, emotional issues, and so on, are all things that can be redefined by the utilization of mind power. Just as a computer formats information into the right sequences, your brain has the ability to do this as well. It does, however, take practice.

Let us think about the power you have to change the world. Yes, you can change the world. Did you know that if you put your mind to it, you could have a profound affect on millions of people? It takes just one person to start a movement. If you don't understand this, simply refer to the Bible. It is a transcription of the force one man had and still, two thousand years later, the effect is growing and prospering.

My intent at this point is to expand your minds to the vastness of what it can create. Most of you are reading this, thinking you could not possibly be as formidable a force as the great Master Jesus. Some of you might be thinking you cannot live up to the representation of Mohammad, Buddha, or Moses. Why not? They all started from humble beginnings. I'm sure if I were present then, I would have been able to see men who were well loved by a few, liked by many, and abhorred by many who did not want to listen to the fact that life could offer more than what they knew. What do you know outside of what you were taught? Why not alleviate yourself of the fear of uncrating your common thoughts and instead, inspire the positive in your world and revile the negativity? Repelling the world of "You can't do it," or from yourself, "I can't do it," is not as difficult as you think.

The pyramids were built one block at a time. A teepee is built one piece at a time. A good home is built on a solid foundation. You have to look at yourself as creating a base that is broad and strong. This, in essence, is your building block. It is your power. It is your seduction of life. You, alone, can overcome all odds. Keep in mind, once again, that you are never truly alone. Your God and Spirit are always available to help lay down the building blocks towards the creation of your new life and direction. This I say to you because I do not ever want you to feel overwhelmed and undermanned. Your mind is the physical part of your ability to infuse this beginning process of exploding into someone you want to be, as well as eradicating the things you don't want to keep. No one can take that ability away from you.

ONE FEATHER

There was a time during one of my incarnations that I was worried about the ruination of the river that ran through our camp settlement. Just like today, hundreds of years ago, people of different backgrounds tended not to always get along. The river problem was created by a rival tribe of Indians who lived further upstream. They were diverting the river for two reasons. The first was to propagate their farm system. The second was more troubling to my friends and me. It was deliberately done with an attempt to have us move from where we lived. They figured if they could reconfigure the flow of the water away from us, not only would it leave us without a sufficient supply for our irrigation needs, but it would also severely diminish our fish source as well.

Many in my community were fearful of doing anything, for in the past, we lost many of our friends and family to the savagery of this opposing tribe. Everyone was afraid to send a force to demand the restoration of the system. For a cycle of thirteen moons, our way of living was diminished and threatened; yet, none of the elders had the gumption to make a stand. The logic was that we were better off with next to nothing, rather than to challenge the negative behavior and end up without anything at all.

I was in my mid-teens at that point, full of vim and vigor. I was also a strong student of the Great Spirit, which simply means that I spent much of my time in reflective meditation and prayer. The blessing given to me was one in that the vision of peace and prosperity was possible if someone would summon up the courage to open a dialogue with the enemy. I felt that this was my calling, my chance to prove that the philosophies of the Great Spirit were both sane and accurate. **Trust** was the feeling given and the advice was to use the power source of my mind.

I went out one day, casting fear and caution to the winds. This was going to be the beginning of a new stage within myself, my life, and the life of all my family and neighbors. As the land moving north passed quickly by my feet, I knew my feat would be seen as epic after all was said and done. Noticing that even the animals that frequented the river were scant, it became more apparent that my mission was not just to turn the minds of my enemies, but to be the speaker of the lower kingdom also. I didn't have a plan when I set out, but I did have some very strong resolve that no matter what it would take, I would trust that my mind wouldn't fail me. At that stage in my life, understanding that I could create something by virtue of what I was thinking, in reality, didn't come into play.

My elders had always told me that if I went anywhere near the rival tribe's camp that they would immediately hunt me down like a fox. As I was walking there, with my hand-raised wolf at my side, it dawned on me that perhaps if I thought like a fox, I would be able to outsmart them. I knew from experience that they were cunning and that the people my family assumed were all bad didn't necessarily value life as much as we did. Also on my mind was the fact that if we did nothing, life amongst my friends and family would continue to vanish. With each footstep closer, the nervousness in my stomach, as well as the resolve within, reached new peaks. There were always several scouts on the lookout for intruders. I was made aware of this by one of my older friends who escaped their wrath with an arrow stuck in his hide. He literally became the butt of our jokes once he recovered.

It was something that weighed heavily on my mind as I alertly forged forward, step-by-step. To my astonishment, a young warrior confronted me. He came across with intent to intimidate me, his bravado not going unnoticed. I knew if he was here that more had to be relatively close by. For some God-known reason, I projected myself as harmless. The warrior backed down a little and this gave my wolf a chance to show that we had the upper hand. My brave animal friend lunged from behind and put my confronter's neck in a toothed grip. The fear in the warrior's eyes was wild and deep. I found myself in a position of control, mostly because I didn't run from this "wolf attack" and instead, moved forward to command the release of the warrior.

He was awestruck by my bravery and grateful for my rescue of him. I sent my gray wolf to the perimeter, using long-worked-on hand signals. The events that came next were rather shocking to me. Out of nowhere, a handful of huge braves surrounded me, having been alerted by the screams of initial fear from their comrade. They all had arrow tips thrusting at me from all angles. I stood my ground, not wanting to show any panic or fear. Briefly, I closed my eyes and envisioned the hand of the Great Spirit intervening. While my lids were still closed, a scuffle ensued and as I came out of my split-second trance, I saw the young man knocking the others away from me. He then explained my magical power over the wolf that attacked him and made it clear that if it weren't for me, he would have gone to the Great Skies.

The next thing that happened was that I was escorted to their settlement. Immediately, I was put in front of the tribal leaders and was told to explain why I had strayed onto their land. This made me very nervous, simply based on stories I had always been told, but my mind stayed positive and focused on what I wanted the outcome to be. There were loud voices shouting at me from every direction. It was an attempt to intimidate me, yet I let it have no affect. Tranquility ran through my body. The eyes of my wolf caught mine from behind the entire ruckus. He knew to stay out of sight unless I needed him.

"Explain yourself!" were the words bellowed.

Now me, who was never at a loss for words, had none immediately available. I stayed passive and then slowly started to speak. What came out of my mouth had nothing to do with my intended mission to get them to remove the series of dams. I'm not sure who was more startled by my confidence and conciliatory words, but it is probably fair to say it was me. Allowing the verbal expressions to flow freely, a story unfurled itself from my lips about **how much better I could make their lives**. Apparently, my listeners were a bit astonished by the brashness of these words, as was I.

It seems that the message that had to be sent to them was coming from someone other than myself, and in fact, it was. My mind was cognizant of what was being said, but it felt as though my mouth was flapping all by itself. Like many of you, I was presumably channeling the confidence from Spirit. The trust that was deeply imbedded was being put to use.

As I gazed past these intimidating people, I noticed that there were many crying children and that the women looked worn-out. Many of the men were coughing and seemed too weak to even move. I recognized that they were going through a health crisis, a plague of sorts. This information was something I learned about from one of my tribal elders a couple of years before. It appeared that this collection of bravado and arrogant people were being punished. Not being that stupid, I never mentioned this to my interrogators.

My first words were, "I know how to fix the disease. I heard rumors of it and wanted to see if you would allow me to help you." This was a distortion of what was told to me for the last year. The elders in my clan would always tell me that the Great Spirit would strike harm to those who intentionally created hardships for others.

"What can one person do?" I was asked. "You have no tools and you have malice in your mind."

I went on to tell them how untrue this was and that

they would be better off if they learned to communicate with their neighbors, rather than to show wanton disregard. "Get to know me and you will see there is no evil intent in my heart or mind."

For some curious reason, they began to ask more and more of what I was thinking. The words flowed freely from me, as I spun a lesson about how they created a dysentery effect when the river was siphoned off. "It is because the natural flow of the water has been disrupted. You have pooled it, and it has become contaminated because it can not run free." I heard those words come out of my mouth and, truthfully, had no idea if they were true or not. There was so much conviction in the pitch of my voice that it sparked many quizzical looks and raised eyebrows.

The next phase of action was that they roughly pulled me towards the interior of their camp. For a split second, I began to think that they were going to kill me off. Then, remembering the importance of the power of my mind thoughts, my head told me all would be well. That didn't keep my heart from feeling like it would thump right out of my chest. Each step seemed to be a mile, which is a clear exaggeration.

I was shown to a couple of other men who seemed to have the responsibility of the raising of the crops. After being told to explain my theory of why they were not being successful, words from my mouth detailed that without the river having clear flow by nature's direction, the Gods were unhappy because of the disruption. I told them because the animal and plant kingdoms were interfered with, that poison was absorbing into the roots of their food. Even though I was unsure of the verity of my discussion, having been schooled many times by the organic specialist in our clan, I knew my words weren't far from reality.

Once my explanation was heard, a tribal conference ensued for several minutes. As it finished, a warrior raced toward me, with an arrow firmly in his grasp. Instead of being frightened, I thrust my chest out for all to see my strength. He looked unhappy, angry, and seemed to have the single purpose of disposing of me on his mind. The tip of his weapon prodded my throat while he screamed. My words to him were simple, but to the others, they were deafening. "I have only come to help you."

With that, he pulled his intimidation tool back and with a frustrating leer, it was released over my head. We spoke many of the same words, but there was different dialect that made for some confusion in translation. An older man came by my side and told me to leave. There was an unspoken glance of thanks and a warning not to be so brash in the future. He told me that the guard that encountered me thought I was sent from the winds of the Gods. My wolf connection was the reason for this. I saw that statement as an opportunity to reestablish contact with my furry friend and yelled a command out as loud as I could. My gray, hairy friend bounded out of the woods and much like a family cat, wrapped my legs with the strength of his body. The looks on the faces of all those nearby was all the gratification I needed as I smiled and turned back to journey home.

It had been a long day for me, starting just at sunup, and not until the sun had sunk behind the far edge of the land did I return home. Several family members and a couple of friends greeted me. All wanted to know where I had gone, and a couple even told me they suspected I was in danger, mostly because of my spirited attitude and sometimes my failure to do things in a conformist way.

Skepticism is the response I received after unwrapping my interesting story to them. There was no sense from any of them that they believed me, nor did they think it did any good. How wrong they would soon find out they were. The proceeding morning, the camp was awakened by shouts of disbelief and joy. Young children were whooping it up, babbling to everyone that the river was running and the fish were jumping once again. It seems that my talk with our antagonist neighbors caused a wave of positive action on their part. They removed the dams and the water took to its natural course again, restoring not only much-needed nutrients to our land, but a full food source supply too. We were going to have a fatted season of prosperity.

I have told you this story for two reasons. You needed to see that if you stay firm in the outcome of what powerful mind optimism can do, it would indeed be just what was needed for you. In my case, not only did it restore hope and joy and end the crisis of impure land and starvation, but also it opened the door to something far greater. Several months later, our homestead was "invaded" by several members of the people I had my talk with.

Although, I was not immediately available when they first approached, no hostilities took place as they made it clear to those who saw them that they were unarmed and meant no harm. The request they came with was to be able to see the "boy-God" that had visited with them. Naturally, this was greeted with some quiet chuckles. My friend, Big Rock, was amongst them and immediately knew they were referring to me. He came to the field I was working in and did a lot of good-natured ribbing about being in the presence of a master. The sarcasm in his voice was not well hidden.

We walked back together, and I felt I would need my wolf friend to be on hand and called for him. As we came upon the congregated cluster, I offered my greetings. The setting was much more relaxed then my first meeting with them. They were on my turf now. As I extended a hand in friendship, some of my own clansmen looked irritated at this gesture. This is when the second great outcome from my journey was given.

One of their leaders reached to the side of his loincloth and handed me a gift. It was meant to be a peace offering. My chief requested to see it and was stunned and impressed that decades of fighting would end without any further bloodshed. Graciously, he accepted the token and sent back with these front men, a gift of acceptance, stained with the blood from his massive, muscular arm as a means of sealing the deal.

Through the confidence and trust I had in and from my mind, we were not only given the gift of restoration of our land, but we would now live in a state of contentment. We would live without the fear and constant edge of worry that had always been there. By simple words, the Great Spirit embraced us with love, protection, and now, a place of honor. It would have been easy for me to let my ego swell, but this was just one of the many lessons in my life that carved the personality and spiritual philosophy that drives me today, even though it is on the side of eternal life.

I was about fourteen years of age when this took place, my voice barely having distinguished itself as belonging to a man. Now, can you see yourselves being able to make a difference in your world? Consider that the tact I took was not one of confrontation, but instead, a showing to those that were opposed to us how to better their own lives. It was a form of deceptive diplomacy and ended years of strife and senseless murders of many innocent people. At a tender age, I was able to accomplish what generations of others much older than I couldn't. You also have the same power over situations when you put your mind to it.

*   *   *   *   *   *

Quietly, someone in spirit continued to talk to me about the success you can have if you go through life with blind trust. Some people might look at that as being a little naïve, but as you will see, Spirit's view might differ. I wish I knew who had given me the following message, but a name was never revealed, although the energy was pure, positive, and sweet.

As often happens to me, the subject took a turn away from where I thought it was heading. Because of my own physical struggles, I couldn't help think that most of this was a direct message to myself, but I was assured it was for all people to hear or read about.

* * * * * *

UNKNOWN SPIRIT—

Now let us move on to another example of how you can empower yourself by minding the power within. There are some people who seem to walk through life always getting things handed to them. This comes despite the fact that you and everyone else might think this person doesn't deserve it. Opinions are not always correct. Bear in mind that I'm not speaking of malicious persons who obtain things by illegal or deceptive behavior. The kind of person I am talking about is the one with the big heart and kind mannerisms.

Suppose you have a young man who appears to struggle all through his elementary and high school education. He squeaks into a college and then begins to outperform anything hc has shown in the past. You might talk to him and still not be able to ascertain the method in which he is being graded on because when you talk to him, the words and scattered thoughts are still present. So, too, is the lack of focus on any conversation, even though it may be a basic and simple topic. You may walk away from him muttering to yourself, perhaps asking, "What's his trick?"

His trick is simple. It is his ability to assume the best for himself. It is his ability to be able to visualize great positions of respect, great amounts of money, and so forth. In other words, he cannot see the negativity of the perception that so many others see in him. In a sense, it is simply having blind faith in his own ability to receive, as well as a complete trust and understanding that his God is helping and protecting him. Maybe the key is that he **expects** to succeed.

What would happen if you learned to have this unabashed attitude? Would success come to you as easily? If you have learned anything up to this point, it is that the truth and value of embracing your aura in a bath of positive thoughts can bring to you what you want. You can just as easily be the same as the young man. You have the ability to breed great things. This greatness I speak of can come in any format. It can be educational, financial, romantic, and spiritual, or any other goal-oriented desire that you have for yourself. You are limitless in potential. Capitalizing on it is what you need to work on.

Sometimes, getting started is the most difficult thing in the world if you allow yourself to become overwhelmed with fear. This can be simplified into a scant few areas. There is fear created by a worry and disbelief that you can do something physically, mentally, emotionally, romantically or financially. Do I sound repetitive? Everything in the universe interconnects.

I will begin by sharing my thoughts about the physical aspect of this. The body is more resilient than most people think. It is also capable of working better and longer if you zero in on the action you want to do by visualizing and developing a plan. What do I mean when I refer to a plan? It is simply to have a minimal starting point, a moderate goal, and an energetic one. The foresight to create adjustments to your most difficult goal is also important.

As an example, perhaps you have not walked in years and your legs are wracked with pain. Maybe it even hurts to move from room to room. For whatever reason, you decide it is time to get yourself in better condition. It could be brought on by general unhappiness, a health problem, or the proverbial midlife crisis. No matter what the reason, you decide that it is the right time to do something, yet your mind inadvertently tells you that you can't do it because of what you know you will feel. The problem with this philosophy is that you are already assuming pain that you haven't felt. We need to eradicate that trend and start looking at things anew.

Before you take your first step towards taking steps to get healthy, goals have to be set before you go anywhere or do anything. Create a mandate for yourself. In other words, have your immediate and average goal all set. It would be preferable for you to put it on paper, since seeing things in black and white has a way of creating reality and finality.

If you are pained when walking, yet know that walking is the best thing for you, begin by writing how many steps or what distance you can go with a fair amount of tolerance. Your goal is to increase it by about ten percent. In other words, if you feel you can walk twenty steps, increase it by two. If you think you can walk a mile, increase it by a tenth of a mile.

Second, you are to be somewhat more aggressive making your moderate goal. If the pain is that bad to begin with, you should say to yourself, "I will walk thirty steps within two weeks." If you aren't bothered by pain so much as inactivity, the method of attack should be, "When I start, I will walk a mile and a tenth, but in a month, I will be walking one and a half miles." The attitude and statement of "I will" is important here because it creates a command in your mind that you have the absolute drive and ability to do this. The more you read this, the more it turns into a mantra. The Great Spirit has given you the gift of success.

Lastly, the aggressive goal should be done with a bit of realism, but at the same time, it has to be far enough away from what you are capable of doing now in order to have significant meaning. Let's suppose you tell yourself you want to be able to walk three miles within three months. It might sound like a lot, but what if you conquer your moderate goal in less than the original time target? The encouragement you get from that should enable you to visualize yourself hitting the three-mile mark without it being a far-fetched thought. You can either move the timing of your goal up, or you can increase the distance, but leave the time at three months. Either way, it gives you a reason to keep pursuing improvement.

Ultimately, by simply prodding yourself and recognizing your achievements, you have put yourself onto a path of physical purification. It is vital that you take time to allow yourself to feel good about **each** of your goals that are met. There is no greater waste of energy than to accomplish something you thought was out of your reach and not take the time to enjoy what you've done. The problem is that by dismissing the answered goal, you have dismissed yourself and its pertinence to your future path of life and liberty. One thing that we, in spirit, want for you to feel and know is that it is symbolic of great rewards when you encase your efforts in a positive light. After all, why did you set a goal to begin with? Wasn't it to make yourself feel better about who you are? After all, how bad can it be to approve of yourself and your success?

I wanted to briefly let you have a taste of the simplicity and ease in which changes can be made. Basically, whether it is exercise or something more difficult to you, the best way to reach your goal is to take one additional step each time you think you've finished. This approach works with physical wellness and eating addictions, as well as a whole host of other areas that give you problems. It can be a rewarding way to increase your patience level.

Let us talk about tipping the scales in your favor so that you don't feel like you are tripping each step of the way through life. To begin with, you must grasp the reality of your weight issues. Are you truly overweight, or is the perception you have of yourself exaggerating it? You must use healthy and **realistic** guidelines to figure out where you want to be in body weight and mass. In this case, don't let your mind dictate your end point without having a smart plan of attack.

Step one is simple: avoid food clichés. I could have said step one is as easy as pie, but that sends a signal that food is your friend, when, in fact, it is your **nourishment**. Food was part of the packaged deal when this great earth was created. It is the sustenance of life. It is meant to taste good, but not to become an entrenched mind process. In other words, you can live well and your food can taste good as long as you adhere to the awareness of not overindulging as a means of comfort. You need to learn to decrease appetite stimulants created by the subconscious mind thoughts. Learn to think in terms of survival, not with the "I'm so hungry I can eat a horse" mentality.

The second step is for you to put yourself in the appropriate frame of mind. You must incorporate what I have been teaching you to this point. Set your goals, set your attitude. For most people, their attitude is the most vital part of conquering their body's possession of extra weight. You must not only be tired of being overweight, but also, you have to stop relying on your weight as a "safety net" for situations—generally social—that you don't think you will fit into. You must be willing to make modifications to your routine. Most people have a hard time understanding that their routine may very well be the basis for weight issues.

You might be asking what I mean by this. It's simple. The human race is a collection of living bodies that program themselves towards specific actions. In general, most are creatures of habits. Most people tend to get up about the same time each day for work, school, or a host of other habitual activities. Generally, meals are eaten around the same time, and we tune into specific periods of the day when **we think** we need a snack or drink. It would be great if you could shake up these timing habits, but the reality is that the physical world often limits this. Basically, I want you to begin when you are ready, not necessarily because your friend or someone else close to you tells you that you have to do something. If it is for medical necessities, all the more reason to get going immediately.

The reason it has to happen when you've decided to improve yourself is that if you do it because of another, the attitude and mind sequence indicates that you **don't** want to. This automatically sets you up for failure. Any diet can be successful if you **want** it to happen. Your approach will be much more optimistic, and your mind power allows you to force changes upon yourself. The road to good health can be as simple as that.

The third step associated with dietary changes is the vitality created when your body gets enough sleep. This is an often-overlooked aspect of weight reduction. Again, it is about putting your mind towards accepting a change in your daily habits. My wish is not to get involved in scientific explanations for any of what you are being taught. Sometimes, the science field does not have enough information about the wonderful ways of Spirit. By gaining a little extra sleep, you enable Spirit to relax your body so that it can function at a higher rate. You may have to sacrifice watching a little television or computer exchanges, but in the end, you will be happy.

The fourth step, in effect, returns us back to the area of physical improvement. The desire to improve yourself must work hand in hand with both aspects. In the dietary sense, you are looking to substitute something not good for yourself with something that is. If it is available to you, your treadmill or exercise bike or equipment must be kept in a convenient and easy to get to location. If it's not convenient, you will be less likely to go to it in the initial stages of your transformation. The reasoning for this is to challenge yourself to use it when you have a craving or desire to put something in your mouth that is not truly necessary. These strong yearnings generally only last a few minutes. During that time, fight the urges by making your body work a bit more. See if you can pedal your way a mile or so and visualize that distance as the distance you have just moved away from the snack you were about to devour.

If it's possible, leave the area and take a walk outside. There's something to be said for absorbing fresh air. It changes the physiology of your body, but more so, it awakens an opportunity to think, visualize, and focus on the reason you are out there to begin with. Somehow, being in nature, no matter how civilized or urban it has become, opens the mental eyes to a new you. Perhaps, you could also say that it is a way for you to come to terms with what you already knew before you started walking.

Our fifth step is one that requires a helper. It is always easier when you have someone to encourage and work with you to achieve your goals. Whether you choose your spouse, friend, child, or professional trainer or nutritionist, you will achieve your goals much easier. They can help keep your mind directed more permanently. Don't be afraid to use any trick you think will help you to solidify your train of mind—or **training of your mind**! It is never a bad thing to have someone encourage you. Sometimes we all need that "kick in the tail" to keep ourselves on the right track—even those of us in spirit!

The sixth creation for you to use is to literally log

your accomplishments. Write down your starting weight and measurements of various body parts. Set it up as an easy to read chart. You will refer to it on a weekly basis so that you can notate the adjustments you are making. No matter how small the change may be, consider it a success. Always keep a positive vibe to your progress, even if you feel like you have faltered to some degree. Failure to do so only reopens old ways of thinking and creates negativity and discouragement. You may find that you might gain a couple of pounds here and there, but if you are true to yourself, your measurements will not necessarily be bad. For those of you who are exercising, this may be likely more frequently in the beginning few weeks. As the body adjusts and becomes more muscle mass, adding a couple of pounds is normal since, in theory, muscle weighs more than fat.

The seventh step is to keep a separate log of every bite of food you put in your mouth. Listing what you drink is also needed, yet water does not have to be written down as long as you are comfortably taking in a healthy amount. We see water as the elixir of life. Make sure you put the time down, and if at all possible, the calorie count. This may actually be the most frustrating activity I have told you about, but it will be the most helpful. Most people tend to think twice when they have to answer to the written image of what they digest. It's harmless in the fact that no one else needs to see what you put down, as you and Spirit are the only ones who know the truth. Essentially, it is a self-monitoring system. In addition, what will transpire from this exercise is that you will see patterns to your eating habits.

There are many times that we are not consciously aware of what we are doing to ourselves. Day after day, you might find that keeping your routine is more important than any disruption, yet in this case, the disruption will be advantageous. It is, and will always be, the answer to redirecting your ambitions towards a higher level. By creating a sense of happiness, the aura you walk with will state that you are supremely confident in yourself. This will then translate into avenues of new opportunities in all facets of your life. You'll be amazed at how quickly things can change when the mind is allowed to do its work.

There are other simple things you can do to help yourself, yet we see some of what might be considered practical as being just the opposite. It is more important for you to trust yourself via the lessons of the mind than it is important for you to deprive yourself. If you have a weakness for a certain type of food, removing it completely from your diet might end up being counterproductive. This isn't to say that you shouldn't avoid it, but instead, what I am trying to teach you is that under the concepts previously outlined, moderation and trusting your new ability to unlock the concepts of the mind will end up being a more helpful tool. One of the ways to do this is by making access to your downfall foods a little more difficult to get at. For instance, if you have a weakness for potato chips, they should be placed in a cabinet that you don't like to go into. Perhaps they should be stored in a cubby that is just out of your reach, or maybe in one that requires you to bend way over or get on your knees to get at them.

What will be repetitive in your mind every time you go to eat some is that the hassle involved, no matter how minimal, becomes a sudden reminder of your desire to make changes. Just that momentary thought is frequently enough to make you leave them where they are and continue to jaunt down the path of better health. Leave foods that are problematic out of eyesight. While the "out of sight, out of mind" mentality is mostly good, sometimes the brain is sending signals of deprivation. When this happens, cravings become stronger and as that yearning continues, you cannot realign your mental thoughts. You end up fighting yourself instead.

Anyone with an addiction, be it alcohol, drugs, food, or anything else, has to come to terms with it in their mind before they can conquer this as the enemy. Chemical dependencies require more psychological work, as well as physical detoxification. It is also more important to learn to maintain a stronger belief and trust in God and Spirit. Food-related problems, in most cases, stem from psychological dependencies. It might be a trigger from childhood, such as depravation of something you really thought you wanted at the time. Instead, by being denied, you carry the need for it all the way into, and many times throughout, your adult life.

Now is the time to change. You can do it! You can overcome all obstacles and deterrents in challenging your own mind and body to become great. We tell you, you are great! It's time to learn how to feel that way. This said, the approach has to be something that you can handle as an individual. Some people need more prompting and support from the outside, yet others are better suited to motivate themselves. The plan of attack you choose has to be something you want. It all starts from wanting to better yourself, and no matter how you choose to do it, the follow-through is vital. **Don't fail to be disciplined in your attempts**. The glory you feel when you can see the effort is being fulfilled will make it all worthwhile.

*　　*　　*　　*　　*　　*

The strength we need in the physical world travels through the veins of the soul.

*　　*　　*　　*　　*　　*

From the tips of the evergreen, the Light of God ignites.
Life gives you more than one choice for everything.
Each day
you must ask yourself if you want to let the
Light travel towards
the trunk and stay anchored, or do you envision
yourself flowing
out from the tips of the tree of life towards
endless possibilities?
Both are required to meet the demands of your
intended happiness.

*　*　　*　　*　　*　　*

One subject that Spirit frequently communicates to me is of of wealth and abundance. My upbringing and the teachings given to me by my parents, schools, and church all seemed to suggest that thinking about excesses was wrong. In my initial days of spiritual opening, all of that was eradicated by what Spirit was intent on teaching me. They made it clear that it was perfectly okay to have great wealth. In fact, I was readily taught how to go about it through repetitive messages of tithing and giving from the heart to churches or organizations that tried to advance spiritualism and God-welcoming beliefs. What follows are just a sampling of the beliefs given to me.

*   *   *   *   *   *

LEONARDO—
ABUNDANCE

This, my people, is a topic in which all normal humans are interested. Abundance and prosperity are keys to survival in the physical world. I hope to be able to shed some light on ways for you to improve your success and overall worth.

Life is about sacrifice and infinite abundance. When you sacrifice or give from the heart, God brings the paths, ways, and means to absorb the love and life you deserve. This simply suggests that one of the primary ways of receiving affluence is by tithing. When you tithe to proper and truly spiritually promoting groups, organizations, or churches, you will be rewarded for this effort. It is important to note that you must give from your heart, not simply because you are looking for a quick way to score monetary success for yourself. To expand on this, as long as you are benefiting by feeling as though you are giving a piece of your love to someone else, then, and only then, will God and Spirit find the right roads to repay or reward you with what you need.

In order to fully understand prosperity and abundance, it is vital for you to recognize that it comes in more forms than simply the accepted definition of money. Prosperity can be shown in the form of money, material items, food, shelter, family, friends, environment, education, and inspiration, but most importantly, it is a form of spirituality. Prosperity is the encompassing aura of your life and the essence of who you are, as well as whom you want to be. So, just who is it that you want to be?

Great opportunities arise all the time. It is with regret that I tell you there are many times that these chances are just summarily dismissed. Many times, they are simply unrecognized for the potential and meaning in which they behold. In time, as you learn how to abide by these swings of creative choices, you become more astute and quicker to allow them onto your everyday path. Basically, it becomes a measure of your true trust and unequivocal devotion to the subtleties of the workings of Spirit.

I am referencing the fact that some of the most potent possibilities may come in seemingly offhand ways. It could simply be that you overhear a conversation about a realistic way to make some extra cash, or it could come as simply as a co-worker offering you some clothes that he or she may not be in need of anymore. In a completely different way, it might be the relevancy of an invitation to join someone at his or her place of worship. Do you really know if you won't fit in or like it before you have witnessed it firsthand? I ask this because people repeatedly lose out on growing experiences simply because they are entrenched in their old way of thinking about things.

Sometimes, we tell you to try to do something new. Sometimes we just reinforce what you already know. The concept behind this is to enlighten you to the multitude of different ways that you can become prosperous. Try not to turn your back on unexpected gifts. Try hard to absorb any uplifting emotion that comes in your direction. Don't make the mistake of dismissing someone's love for you simply because you are afraid it might not work out. This goes back to what I have been saying. How do you know that a particular person is not only true in their feelings for you, but might also end up being the most fun and prosperous path you should align yourself with? Keep in mind, it is not all about financial wealth, but more about making your souls feel like they can soar to new and exciting places.

Let us examine freedom of the soul for a moment. Is it living without law? Is it about being able to do anything you want without fallout from others? Or perhaps, is it about absorbing the power and tranquility in abundance that a Higher Power has to offer you? From our point in spirit, clearly it is all about accepting the prosperity that comes when you allow your soul, your inner self, and your actions to be enlightened by something that is admittedly hard to see at times. I say this because through the media and exposure to people in general, if we cannot have a solid, physical image of something, it becomes hard to allow the mind to embrace it.

Do yourselves a favor and stop overanalyzing everything that you come in contact with that differs from what you feel comfortable with. The essence of what I am telling you is quite simple. It is all about being free to worship and trust that following a path of higher intelligence will ultimately and undoubtedly lead to abundance in your lives. There are so many ways to measure abundance that it is hard to include them all here.

We could begin with the value that is received from someone who is in tune with a direction that includes the power and concept of God in their everyday existence. There is no easier way to become successful than with the awareness and acceptance of the Supreme Being in your pocket. We were given life. This, in itself, is a bounty of fruition, hope, and wealth on more levels than anyone can imagine. It gives you the right to seek and capture happiness, love, success, intelligence, hope, desire, leadership, and much more. It gives you the right to anticipate; yet, we strive to teach you that anticipation should be used in a more positive method.

With that said, God has created a life for you that is full of privileges and one where Spirit tries to get rid of the angst that many people feel in their day-to-day activities. The pleasures of what you can have are always around you. What is needed is for all people to be observant of it. In the animal kingdom, clarity is prevalent at all times. Our four-legged friends have learned to simplify their need for abundance simply by trying to gain only what is available for consumption. I use this as a means of teaching all of you that minimal consumption actually creates a fatted and happy life. This is not a statement that you should not seek better things for yourself. It is one in which if you learn to live within your means, advancement opportunities that create more joy in the future are easier to achieve.

Achievements breed more achievements. One never knows exactly where their path will take them, yet the honor we feel in accomplishing a great feat on a personal level has ramifications that exceed even our most realistic expectations. Your confidence will soar and your excitement that life does hold rewards increases. Happiness is one of the most powerful gifts you can give yourself. That is why you should not readily turn down unexpected opportunities when they present themselves to you. It could be one of the many ways that God tries to send a gift of abundance to you.

Let us continue with the thought of the gift of impoverishment. Yes, that can also be seen in a roundabout way as a form of abundance. From the point of being penniless, you can obtain a unique perspective on some of the simpler joys of life. The person who may be considered poor by many, may be blessed with the ability to look at good health as being something special. As simple as that sounds, it is a truism. People tend to ignore aspects of life such as this when they don't worry about how they will pay for something if they get ill. Those who don't have financial means look at the fact that they don't have a doctor, prescription, or hospital bill as something to be happy about. It is their aspect of what may feel like prosperity to them. It also should be a reminder of the vast differences that the multitudes in society see as what is or is not infinite abundance and wealth.

*   *   *   *   *   *

The time of year that last message was given to me apparently had great significance to them. I was interrupted by their desire to send forth a special holiday message. My mind was open to it, as learning about anything Spirit wants to converse about is always of interest to me. Although the message was still supposed to be about abundance, it came through in a very thought-provoking manner. You will see what I mean as you continue to read.

One of the most extreme, known, and perhaps misunderstood ways that God has presented us with opportunities may come from the history of the crucifixion of Jesus. Let me share the following with you:

*   *   *   *   *   *

AN "EASTER" MESSAGE

Many people throughout the world see the resurrection of Jesus as being the most holy and pure day of the calendar year. It is symbolic, though, of the abundance that the God Master has given us. It allows each of us to have comfort, safety, and freedom rise within our souls and our hearts.

During this holy time, I must ask you not to look at this as one day, but rather invoke it as the meaning of your life. You were given an opportunity to come close to a high spiritual entity. The reference we make here is that as each of you go about your daily chores—with many of you not giving a thought at all to the fact that you are free to do so—that throughout history, a struggle for peace and freedom has gone on and is highlighted by the killing of Jesus Christ. There are no other recorded instances as profound as this in which someone openly and readily availed their soul so that others may be consecrated.

In spirit, we follow a truly nondenominational path to life. We are unopposed to any religious facet as long as these sects have pure and well-meaning intentions. We do not want war to be a measure of peace, yet sometimes in our lives, the opposite of exactly what we want takes place. In the current global society, struggles are occurring in many parts of the world. You have the ability to be opposed to it, yet, at the same time, we wish that you would invoke your prayers and speak your mind as to how important freedom and justice is.

I have used the word "invoke" a couple of times because all people have the ability to call forth their power, their energies, their prayers to the highest and most supreme beings. You have the right to pray as you see fit, but at the same time, you must understand that others throughout the world have the right to pray as they see fit. This day marks an egregious and heartbreaking

113

tragedy. At the same time though, it is the recognition of everlasting life. As you move forward throughout your daily transition, I ask that you take a moment here and there to reflect on the greatness of whom you are and most certainly, on the greatness of your God. You must not look at the crucifixion of Jesus Christ as a symbol of hatred amongst men, but instead, see it as enlightenment to those who truly do not understand, because God created all of mankind in His image.

Please understand that perfection is a piece of your soul, but your physical lives make it nearly impossible to be perfect yourselves. That is why constant striving forward is on the everlasting agenda. We see all of you as great beings. We see all of you with the fullest potential and with the deepest amount of love and respect possible. We see that many of you are suffering from illnesses, be it physical or emotional. We see that some of you are struggling with your spiritual concepts of what life is meant to be. In spirit, we understand that romantic situations may not always fall on the path that you want; yet, we embrace the idea of physical, eternal togetherness. We want for you to be able to be free to love someone so deeply and so firmly that there are times you may cry from the depths of the emotions when you look at your partner.

For those of you who seem to maintain a path of solitude, we in spirit shed our tears for you from the love and respect we have *for* you and hope that you have for yourself. I ask for you, in the memory of your God and yourself, to take a few moments to show gratitude for what you do have, to show respect for the abundance and for the infinite number of opportunities that you are receiving. May the bounty of Christ and the bounty of love you are given be yours today, tomorrow, and forever.

*　　*　　*　　*　　*　　*

*Come unto me all my children. I will treat you
fairly and with love.
Desertion from the flock of mankind is,
and should always be, done
only with the true acknowledgement of the
God King. Center
yourselves as the true Christ Beings that all
of you are. Pray for
peace through your temples, mosques,
dojos, synagogues, or churches,
but always through your representative heart.*

*　　*　　*　　*　　*　　*

ONE FEATHER—

During one of my incarnated lives, I went through a stretch of time where food was scarce. Many of our people were falling ill to the weaknesses that come to the physical body when it is deprived of nourishment. I watched with unwanted intensity as many of the elders uncharacteristically and unconsciously moaned from their hunger pains. Children cried and even the nursing infants were wailing because they couldn't draw enough milk from the breast of their mothers.

It was an unusually arid summer, and the drought carried into the fall. Even the leaves of the trees began to drop off early. Dehydration in many areas was being felt. Our food sources were taking a beating. Both our fields of edible greens, squash, and corn, and our prairies and leas that normally were home to the animals we hunted werc basically barren. We worried as the winter season would soon be upon us, and we didn't have the reserves prepared to carry us through what was the traditionally hardest time of year for us to deal with. Famine seemed to be gripping our community. I witnessed a look of fright and despair in the eyes of many people, especially those mothers with small children. Seeing them made my own panicky fears seem unfounded.

I'm relaying this story to you for a specific reason. Sometimes, until we have normal situations change, our abundance in life is not noticed. We went years without worrying about how we would eat or drink. Even during what we previously thought were hard times paled in comparison to this seasonal stretch. The lack of food for the animals ended up being a lack of food for us. It also meant that our skins were not as plentiful and that affected everything from the walls in our homes to the clothes we made to keep ourselves safe from the elements.

In your lives, abundance is often overlooked. Many people who are accustomed to having most of their needs filled all the time tend to dismiss that this is actually a form of prosperity. It is not something that should be taken lightly. In fact, I am asking all of you to take a reflective look at your standing in life. Do you show gratitude to anyone for what you have? Do you simply assume that you deserve all that you have? Are you aware of the millions of people throughout the country and world who are not remotely close to having the same benefits that you have? What have you done to assist others less fortunate? Have you donated your resources, including your time, to help any of them?

Out of all those questions, the one I view as most important is the one in which you might think that you deserve everything you have. For some, my answer may surprise you. It is well within your essence to have all of it. You do deserve it! The Great Spirit wanted everyone to have excesses, but the key to all of it continuing is in how you share it with others. To open your stream of generosity creates an unending flow of good things back to you.

Let us begin by repeating to you that there is a true need from Spirit to see that you are grateful for what you have and what you receive. It has been told that the law of abundance is simply giving back ten percent of what you have to spiritually promoting churches or groups whose **pure intentions** are about increasing the work and connections to and through the Higher Power. If you can become accustomed to doing this, "the law" states that the gift you give will be returned in one form or another as much as tenfold to your tithing. This simply means that if you give one dollar you should expect to get back as much as ten dollars. None of this will yield itself to you if the offering or tithing does not come from your heart.

Perhaps the easiest way to reach your goals is through an unyielding devotion to the belief that you deserve and trust in the Great Spirit's devotion to your own well-being. It is easy for anyone to claim they are God-abiding citizens, but it is not always as simple as saying those words. In actuality, it takes practice to achieve unison with pure thoughts and an optimistic overview of life at all times. This is simply because the human specimen is just that—human. Spirit docs not expect total perfection in anything you do. Rather, **we desire perfection from you**. You see, we have more trust in your abilities to succeed than you do in yourselves. That is precisely why your mission on earth may seem so complicated and unfair. Those of us in spirit and around you assume greatness, as well as great things for and from each person.

Can you imagine how easy it would be for you to reach what you see as the pinnacle of achieving your goals when you embed the thought of simple, divine intervention into every effort you make to accomplish something? Again, one of the common threads to personal success is to look at your goals and thoughts and decide that the best and fastest way to bring them to you is through the philosophy of "Keep It Simple." Not only will you be given the riches you deserve, but your healing powers within your own body, your mental and emotional makeup, and your spiritual strength will all benefit. How nice would it be for you to go through life feeling less discomfort in all facets of living.

I have just made it seem like this is a very easy thing to do. In theory, it is, but in practical use, it is something that requires persistence and mental domination—mind power—over all those negative thoughts and images that creep into your head. You can overcome the "I can't do it" impressions that were pressed into you from people who had a profound impact on your personality as children.

It appears to me that I have been shifting this talk of abundance towards the fascinating scheme of what it takes for true happiness to fall into play for everyone. I suppose that the most difficult thing for anyone to do in the physical plane is to override the negativity and doubt that was unfairly and inaccurately cast upon you. There are many things in life that can disrupt your quest for completion, beginning with parents who inadvertently have inferior thoughts, to teachers and friends of the same beliefs. The great thing about all of this is that at any time you put your mind to the task, you can change all of what you are unhappy about at virtually any age. It is never too late to embrace the sound fundamentals of living in a spiritual vortex of enlightenment. The fastest way to get to where you want to be is to practice, practice, and practice again, the values of all the things we are teaching you. Through perspiration and perseverance, abundance does not need to be a foreign entity. Be a warrior and attack all the issues that you feel threatened by.

*   *   *   *   *   *

A personal favorite topic of mine is when any one of the handful of spirits that I channel on a regular basis gives me insight or some other thoughts about animals. I am warmed by the fact that even though our society has been so disrespectful to the other creatures and life on earth that Spirit hasn't forgotten how to govern and press for their protection. This next segment was given to me in a very fast, informative, and forceful way.

Hopefully, you will gain the depth of the message that I did while I was receiving these comforting words. It definitely gives all of us in the flesh something to think about.

*   *   *   *   *   *

ONE FEATHER— ANIMALS

Our view on animals is that they can bring joy, levity, and assist in the healing of all people. It is our sense and awareness that most of those on the earth plane actually don't understand the balance between the kingdoms of man, plant, and animal. For now, we will discuss the strength of having animals in your lives on a few levels.

First and foremost, animals as pets, when kept properly, are a gift for you. It is a gift for them, and the Great Spirit sees it as a gift for Spirit. Simply put, to have a dog, a cat, a horse, or whatever animal gives you joy and allows you to have a feeling of achievement and accomplishment. There is something that happens between the souls of yourself and your pets. A bond of trust is formed. No other relationship can assimilate the same feelings. Often, people don't recognize the importance of this union until it is taken away.

Now, I have said that for a reason. It is to get each of you to spend a few moments to think about what your life would be like without your pet. Would there be loneliness? How many of you would come to realize how many subtle actions on your part revolve around your friend? I think it is fair to say that most everyone would be surprised by the smallest things, perhaps as simple as looking under the recliner to make sure that your friend is not in the way. Their feeding schedules become commonplace and are more of a habit for you than they might be for your furred one. You might find yourself momentarily glancing down the hall or in a corner for an animal that is taken from you suddenly. Animals play a strong subconscious role in your daily movements.

There is the same sense of loss for a pet when it dies as there is when your fellow man dies. This is said to get you to understand that it is not silly or foolish to feel like you are grieving too much. In fact, because of the nondemanding relationship you can have with a pet, it is more likely that you will feel greater sadness than if a friend passes. This is seen as normal by Spirit. For myself, I see it as an accomplishment of the life that your pet had. It shows how valuable the bond between both of you was forged. It shows respect. It shows an awareness of life on the most basic level, in which your God created an opportunity for both souls to unite to help each other. By compassionately embracing a love from an animal that wants nothing more than to be loved, you have answered in many ways the animal's reason for being here. You have also allowed yourself a chance to be loved without feeling like you are obligated for anything more.

Perhaps the bond between men or women and animals is the most basic relationship you can ever have. It does something more when this association happens when you are young. It teaches you how to have a good relationship with someone who can be very different from you. Tolerance and compassion for life is etched into the soul and the person. You are being taught the best lesson in life: unadulterated love. At the same time, the valuable lesson of trust is also forged. This trust is something that animals have to have if they want to survive, but humans need to develop it to ensure permanent awareness of safety in the world as they see it. It helps to relieve people of unnecessary phobias.

The love of an animal can be healing. Inspiration to overcome illnesses and fears, or maybe fear of an illness, is easily taken from the simplicity of a "kiss" from a dog, the purring of a cat, the neighing of a horse, the cooing of a bird, and so on. The mechanism built into each of us is that animals, in most cases, are not a threat and don't want us to do things we can't do or aren't ready to try. There is an unspoken communication that many animals have with us. It is responsible for giving us courage and the feeling and sense of safety to explore the world beyond the barriers that we put up for ourselves or that others teach us to have. This is why barriers to healing are broken down. Hopefully, in the future, doctors will further ingratiate themselves with this knowledge and share it with their patients.

All people in the physical world need to be the caregivers for nature. Without the quality of good intent and a union with the minds of animals, life's balance will change. For centuries now, people have forgotten that they are intruding on nature and nature is not violating the space of people. As simple as that is, most everyone doesn't look at it that way. The creation of the Great Spirit was one of perfection, harmony, and balance amongst all levels of souls. People must create a stronger voice to protect the boundaries of wildlife. All nature is part of the complete plan and deserves to be spoken for.

There is another factor that does not go unnoticed by those of us in spirit. Sometimes, regeneration needs to take place in order to stabilize and revitalize the good of nature. Pruning, or taking down trees in a spot that is too small for them to live freely, actually opens the opportunity up for other types of animals and plants to flourish. It also allows for the replacement, or "rebirth," of the same types so that smaller creatures can manifest and mark their existence by cohabitating and growing with it.

We do not refer to constant advancement of the coastline and forest for personal gains as the same event as what I just mentioned. Clear-cutting the trees just for the use of its timber or to allow for lush, sprawling lawns with no purpose other than showing a panoramic view of wealth is not the same as trimming something to make room for new growth. Animals need a place to feel safe. Are you creating that for them?

When was the last time you changed something on your property or someone else's and thought about how it would impact the present life that was attached or living in the trees or shrubs? Better yet, were you able to have the foresight to see the excitement of small animal bodies that were reveling in the fact that they had a new dominion? Small changes create a wave of new chances for animals that may not have had a chance to survive otherwise. My message here is that thoughtless, selfish change is no good, but change with the concept of revitalizing an area is outstanding. Some shifting in location forces animals to be cognizant of their survival and makes them work harder for it. This, according to the animal Gods and Spirits, makes them viable to continue to survive through the evolution of the earth. Animals will be on this planet long after man has disavowed the plan of the Great Spirit and caused its destruction.

If that sounds a little scary, then I have made my point. If all people don't take the time to recall and live through the simple foundations of love, sharing, and prayer, then devastation will take hold. On the other hand, if all people learn to work in unison and with resolve that is full of good and pure intentions, the end of the world, as we know it, does not have to be. Change is imminent. It attaches to everything, both man, woman, plant, and animal. Learn to diversify your thoughts and talk or pray for salvation. It is the quickest way to develop "blind trust" in the Great Spirit, just in the same way animals live all the time. It is ironic that what they have to fear most is the same thing that mankind has to fear most—man.

All people must learn about the soul connections with the animal world. There is a deep-seated magnetism that allows animals to bond with their human counterparts. Sometimes it cannot be explained in physical plane terms, but the essence of the cause is that they have a soul that is automatically trusting of the souls of mankind. The problem with that is that over centuries, they have had to learn to protect themselves, not just because many of them end up as part of the food chain, but also because they have seen their wilderness ravaged by selfishness and greed. Where do you fit in? Are you one of those people who unthinkingly kills off any animal in sight just for the fun of it, or are you more aware of the need to protect them? The protection is with the animals' best interest in mind, not yours.

That said; it is vital that people start to incorporate this value into their human residences. How hard is it for you to leave a corner of your property—or much more— in a natural state so that the loving creatures from the kingdom of animals can feel secure? Sometimes men and women try so hard to make their property perfect that they forget that no matter how small a gesture, there is always a way to return something to the animal world. You can leave food, bedding material, places to hide, and so forth if you really want to make a difference. Ponds for fish and plants also work as a food source for predators and birds. Many of them can be attracted to pesky insects trying to incubate in the water. By using the larvae and insects as a food source, it helps keep your personal environment more comfortable.

In my mind, while I was relaying these words to you, I recognized that insects are part of the animal kingdom as well, but for the purpose of this message, the focus was on anything that fell outside the insect world. Besides, bugs are the most resilient creation that God has made. They have learned to adapt to virtually any type of surrounding over centuries of man's "progress."

*   *   *   *   *   *

Like the dove that symbolizes divinity, your soul can soar too.

*   *   *   *   *   *

*Freedom and peace can be achieved
only when oppressors turn
blind towards the ignorance of their own
philosophies and
open their hearts to sensible freedom and
peace for all. Sometimes,
they need help seeing this. Are you prepared
to teach them?*

*   *   *   *   *   *

When Spirit speaks to me, a variety of emotions, thoughts, and physical feelings overtake me. Most of the time, I feel in complete control and never really give the words much thought as they flow through me. The following message—short story—was given with an immense force. At times when I was channeling it in, my body felt as if it were shaking, and I could feel a surge of love burrowing deep inside.

As you will see, not all of the messages are as easy to forecast as you think. This one, in particular, threw such a curve that I felt awestruck by what happened. One of my biggest reasons to feel upset with anything is when I can't convey the strength and ultimate power of the energy that Spirit graces me with. Hopefully, all of you will acknowledge the same sense of awareness and love that I did the first time I "heard" these words.

*   *   *   *   *   *

UNKNOWN SPIRIT—

On one fine day, my eyes opened to see the gloom of the sky and to feel the aches of dampness in my bones. The air was heavy with humidity; the sound of people screaming at each other pierced my auditory senses. I could smell the noxious odors of rubber burning as a car must have gone up in flames nearby. Gunshots could be heard in the background, and frantic screeches of despair from those close to it resonated into my soul.

Today was my next chance to embrace this surrounding, to do my small part to bring smiles to as many of the downtrodden as I could. Momentarily, my mind let me slip into a thought pattern of a frustrated "Here we go again," then as usual, the spirit of myself used that negativity to ignite the passion that was always burning within. Today, I would change the world for the better!

I washed the death off my face, dressed, and playfully

slapped myself to invigorate me for the task at hand. As the door to my apartment closed, the entrance to the urban blight and malaise opened. This made me happy, which by most standards, probably sounds crazy. No matter where I turned, impoverishment was the only thing that seemed abundant. There were days when I wondered why it was so important to me to seek a way to spread an enlightened and hopeful way of looking at life to as many as I could. The children were the key to future change. My mark would be left on them as I knew that with some consistency and obstacle jumping, they would start to absorb my attitude for themselves—even if understanding it might not come for years.

I lightly stepped around the trash that always seemed to pile up and avoided walking too close to the dead, diseased rats that were strewn about. Sometimes, they seemed to be as abundant as the paper left after a ticker-tape parade. I glanced at the homeless, making sure I flashed each of them a hearty smile and a heartfelt hello. Many of them responded with the same, albeit, with lesser energy than mine, but that was okay. Unbeknownst to most of them, that exchange *gave them hope* for their day.

My walked continued past the graffiti-marred buildings, past the stripped cars, past the burned-out remnants of an apartment complex. As my steps carried me forward, I witnessed an attack that was about to happen. This is when my pace slowed down. A surge of loving energy vibrated through my body, the intensity so strong that I knew I had the strength to intercede to prevent it, despite my diminutive physique. I knew that

God would be with me. He always was.

I approached the fierce-looking male that was just about to hustle the young woman into an alleyway. His target looked as though she saw an angel. He looked as though he were baffled that anyone would have the courage, and in his mind, the stupidity, to come near him. It was at that moment that a fight ensued, but it was a fight within himself. I motioned to the teen girl to sit for a minute, which she did, more because she was still petrified and couldn't get her legs to move.

The rage of this perpetrator was trying to erupt again. There was a lot of cursing and ranting, but the words were meaningless to me. Long ago, I learned not to let the negative orations of others enter into my head. It was a gift from God to be able to do that; otherwise, I'd be just like almost all other humans. Then, with the quickness of a lizard's tongue, he tried to strike me, but I was impervious to it. The young lady watched with amusement as this attempt continued repeatedly. Our person with the evil thoughts began to get more and more frustrated as his futile flailing continued, his mind now echoing with voices within, keeping him at bay.

Finally, he surrendered. It began to become apparent to him that his will wasn't going to outlast mine. Sadness ran through him. The realization that he misspent the life that was granted to him suddenly became evident. His sorrow began to flow in an avalanche of tears. His voice rang out with, "God, what have I done? Why have You let me fall into the hell my life has become?"

The young lady now rose up, no longer afraid of her attacker. She instinctively went to him to offer her hand in a great show of strength and support for this wretched person. Only moments before, she was shaking with fear of him, but something inside her changed too. She felt the presence of God. Now, here I stood beside two people who felt the same thing. A sense of smugness ran through me, knowing that they knew what I knew for so many years had just been transferred to each of them. My job was done for that moment.

I was able to see the future now. The bad man would become so aware of the gift he was given that he would begin immediately to dismantle the minds of the kids who were being bribed by the allure of gang life and show them that hope was the way they could improve their futures. The young woman would become a teacher of life and for life, showing others that even in their darkest moments, a love would be available for them to absorb. The lesson for both of them ended up being the same. Each one not only now believed that a better tomorrow was available, but they **knew** it was.

It was time for me slip away from that scene as unnoticed as I came upon it. My energy would take me to new areas to repeat similar awakenings. As the two of them looked towards me, my Light appeared strong; my resolve would stay with both of them for the rest of their lives. Such is the outcome when God speaks to each of you through angels from heaven and earth. Trust in the Power.

*   *   *   *   *   *

Usefulness comes from tiring of uselessness.

*　　*　　*　　*　　*　　*

The theory behind relativity is that we all connect.

*　　*　　*　　*　　*　　*

Boosting the morale of others should do the same for yourself if you embrace it.

*　　*　　*　　*　　*　　*

EGYPTIAN—

This is a simple message, but one that needs to be paid attention to: Advice is something that is often not asked for but frequently given. Embrace the notions of different ideas. Personal growth comes when you allow your horizons to expand.

Consider that just as the winds of life can blow a ship off-course, you, too, can have the sails of your existence manipulated by greater forces. What you do with the challenge will determine if you are versatile enough to go with the flow. Adjustments are part of all lives. Remember, a wise man once told me, "Make sure if you are going to drop your anchor that your feet are not in the way."

*　　*　　*　　*　　*　　*

These next few messages were definitively requested

131

by Spirit to be included in the selection you have been reading. Although they all have meaning to me personally, it became apparent that they would have completely different translations for everyone who reads them.

LEONARDO—

I have always found it interesting that even people who are on strong spiritual paths are always searching for God. You look high and low. You look for it in some form of special awareness, a grotto, out at sea. It is searched for in churches and in all places of sanctuaries. God is looked for in homes, perhaps in signs within your home. Many seek a special event or a dramatic occurrence. Most people end their lives feeling as though they were not successful in finding His presence.

I am here to tell you that you have been searching for no reason. The God Energy is in EVERYTHING! It is in you, your pets, houses, gardens, cars, kids, and friends. God is in your breath, your way of life. He is in the art forms that are enmeshed in all people, all souls. Beauty is God. Health is God. Illness might be part of God. Breath is God.

Now, I have said this for a few reasons. In spirit, we try to encourage you to see the goodness, the kindness in life and people. Most though, overcomplicate the connection. All you need to do to be happy in life is to accept that part of your soul that is the High Energy. Somehow, you must learn to trust the divinization that is so strongly available and immersed within.

Finding God is not about how many people you can convert to your way of thinking. It is not about doing evil things and claiming it is in the name of God. It is not about showing up at church every day or week to prove to others how devout and religious you are. God is about *acceptance*. It is about seeing the joys that touch everything in your life: a toddler's giggle, a soft kiss from your lover, maybe even that you drove safely to the corner store because you had the protection and a piece of infinite abundance to enable you to do that. God is found when you recognize the value of family, good and pure morals, the excitement of a sporting contest.

Sometimes, it is even about wisdom. Why is wisdom separate from the other examples? It is because wisdom and a consistent desire to learn and create more awareness and discernment about your life and environment is what leads to actually feeling the Highest Power. Wisdom is what we seek for the soul. It directly leads to many of the lessons that the soul needs to learn in order to absorb total cosmic knowledge. It is about spinning out from the God within us to become a complete piece of this Energy.

Now it is up to you to stop searching and simply start accepting that God is already in your life. Be secure in the awareness that each breath you take, each step you make, is assisted by the omnipresent abilities of God. Capitalize on the importance of who you are and what you mean to the greater consciousness of the universe. Make sure you understand that you are a huge part of the "phantom" Creator. Truly though, I have now made you wiser to the fact that each movement in life and everything attached to it is completely and lovingly enveloped by the strongest symbol of God—yourself!

*   *   *   *   *   *

*For I am the angel sent before you; I, Gabriel,
will lead your
path to good health and prosperity. Pray to me.*

*   *   *   *   *   *

*Life is a choice. Either you live it or you endure it.
Preference to the positive can mean everything.*

*   *   *   *   *   *

ONE FEATHER—
CONNECTING

Each person has the ability to feel the presence of the Great Spirit, regardless of how advanced they may feel they are spiritually or in a religious context. I speak of the clarity one gets when they sit quietly or just accept the environment as it is. In this state of being, you can feel the air change. The lighting seems to become more pure and for many people, there is a golden hue to it.

This was the case for me on one fine day. I set off to do some deep thinking, some reflective meditating. There were stresses in my life that I didn't want to contend with, even though I instinctively and academically knew they weren't going away. These were usually the times in my life that I would find an insatiable desire to be with the earth Gods. It gave me a sense of peace and comfort that is ordinarily hard to achieve during normal awareness.

Upon reaching my destination—a field that rambled between a large lake on one side and a beautiful stream on another, with the mountain air gently blowing from afar—I sat down. There was a huge, mighty oak tree that I liked to sit near or against at times, depending on how many ants were working it. Having these small creatures of labor crawling all over me was not conducive to allowing me to clear my mind and allow for the images of God to come to me.

My body took a seated position, but I felt myself leaning back more and more until I was prone. I stared at the sunlit sky, admiring the gentleness of the puffy clouds and the depth of the blue backdrop. Smiles came across my face as I witnessed birds of all kinds flying with an urgency that only they themselves knew what it was for. Butterflies danced past my view, some simple white, others with more elaborate color schemes. The more I relaxed, the more I became in tune with the sounds of life that seemed to be reaching melodic decibels. The music put me in a state of existence that I had hoped would happen.

My body soon felt as though it were floating. My eyes were now closed and except for an occasional peek to see what the world around me looked like, I was overcome with spiritual sensations. I felt like I was one with the earth. A sense of knowing that I was part of this living and breathing planet made me feel emotional beyond normal feelings and thoughts. I could sense a oneness with the Great Spirit and felt that a communication was taking place that wasn't hampered by words or gestures. It was pure, powerful, and positive.

The presence of enormous energies flowed through me, making me feel insignificant in the larger picture. Somehow, my body was absorbing the tones of colors, which may sound silly, but I was aware that they wrapped around me in ways that made me feel safe and free of all my fears and concerns. Although my body was lying in a field, I had the enviable sense of floating high above it, protected only by the hand of salvation that I knew could only come from the Great Spirit himself. Words were exchanged without voice, without sound. This was a communication of the highest form. It was both reverent and human at the same time.

I felt compelled to open my eyes. Upon doing so, the blue sky seemed to be speckled with gold flecks amongst the jumping colors of the rainbow. It amazed me. How could the world have changed right before my eyes? Was I hallucinating? Did I take too many inhales on the opium pipe? Was I dreaming? Did death take me? My mind was momentarily panicking, but a feeling of tranquility grabbed me again, one that I never wanted to let go of.

This was the same scenario that had played out many times before. It was my retreat and at the same time, it was a treat to feel like I was in the presence of the Great Spirit. Information would be exchanged in a subconscious form that allowed me to have the answers and courage to deal with the physical world problems that plagued me. Life wasn't that bad after all. Handling the adversity of dying relatives, sick friends, and evil-minded, lurking neighbors always seemed to disappear. It was as though I were in the womb of Mother Earth, where the sounds of life from trees to bees were buzzing loudly. The sweet sounds of birds, the calls of wildlife were intensified. My hearing was magnified, as was my sight, but my eyes were closed most of the time. I would marvel at the fact that I could actually hear the life of the trees. Popping sounds from the leaves and sap reverberated in my ears.

This was an experience that was available to me on any given day that I wanted. Sitting quietly enough to trust the powers of the Holy One was the key to absorbing into His presence. It is also available to all of you. Let your minds go deep enough into your own prayerful and meditative state so you can experience it. Don't be afraid of feeling like you are soaring above your body. Let your mind succumb to the pleasantries of God's desire. Be of the mind that you want and accept the station of peace and nobility that you deserve. Have your body immerse with the power of nature. Absorb, absorb, and absorb more of it. Allow yourself to see the changes in the environment and bless the ability for new life to take its place.

What I have described to you is the foundation for bonding with your God. There is no right or wrong way to do this. It is about being comfortable with yourself, feeling safe beyond ordinary thoughts so that you can be naked in the loving arms of the Highest Power. There are many ways to receive this impression. You don't need to lie in a pristine field, nor sit in a place of holiness. It is an attainable action no matter where you are. The key is to be gentle enough in how you receive your surroundings and accept what your own comfort zone is. Try to establish a place that is void of noise and discomfort.

Once you alleviate the useless actions of worrying and stressing, a sense of belonging to a bigger and broader range of life will start to seep into your soul. The truth is that it is already there, but you need to take advantage of it instead of ignoring the presence of the universe and the Great Spirit. By allowing this event to take place time after time, slowly at first, your conscious thoughts will recognize that "beating yourself up" is counterproductive to establishing days filled with happiness.

Isn't obtaining happiness what all of us want, whether on the side of Spirit or in the physical realm of life? If you can let yourself go, let your mind be free of physical world content, then you can achieve the same sense of purpose and peace of mind, heart, and soul that you seek. Whenever I found myself in the zone of life that *was spirit*, all the issues that weighed heavily on me would seem to be unimportant and useless to dwell on. The fog of my mind would disappear, and I would feel lighter, both literally and figuratively. I cannot begin to tell each of you that the essence of oneness you feel when in the presence of the Great Spirit is unequaled to anything or any amount of love that you can muster up.

Perhaps I can better explain that the feeling I am trying to convey to all of you is a feeling of purity, power, and promptness. The purity comes from the level of love that wraps its energy around you. It is not something that can be ordinarily felt in the regular course of life. It is not something that you can turn on or off, although people of high spiritual values and awareness are able to do so more regularly. It is, however, something that can be learned, but never forced.

The power is a reference to the complete feeling of control you have over your own dominion. You are able to sense possibilities and abilities to bring to you all the things you were afraid weren't truly available. You are able to conceptualize and visualize all the goods facts that you want for yourself. As I have already said, this power makes you feel as though you are in control of your physical destiny. Learning will come easier in the future, and disparaging thoughts will diminish.

Promptness will come from a speedy implementation of using the feelings of what you sense when you are in a state of peace with God. In other words, if you put aside old ways of thinking before you enter into the tranquility of the Light that is available to your souls to embrace, future actions and wishes will form and conceptualize in the literal sense.

May you all be blessed with the white Light, the Light of the Golden Kingdom.

*   *   *   *   *   *

Validation is something that only needs to be done for humankind. Trust is a gift of the soul. Allow your soul to be the guiding Light.

*   *   *   *   *   *

Solace of the mind comes from the heart.

*   *   *   *   *   *

LEONARDO—

One of the most difficult things for anyone to do is to reflect on their own reflection. Take the time to see who you are. Life will become more balanced for you as you learn to trust and change the imagery in your mind when it comes to how you see yourself. Your personality is your canvas. By working with it, you can create beautiful things. Optimism for your future is in your hands, in your control. Imagine how powerful you can be when you ingrain the colors of life that you want yourself to be. It is an awesome experience to feel blessed by the fabric of yourself.

While this sounds odd, I know for a fact from the side of Jesus that a legacy can be left for centuries when you don't antagonize the simple pleasures of seeing yourself as the blessed, beautiful, and bountiful mosaic that God created within you. You are an art form of indelible and everlasting meaning. Knowing this, are you going to embrace the personality that you want to be, or will you fester in insecurities and an unsteady vision of yourself for millenniums to come? It seems to me that most people tend not to be confident enough in themselves to elaborate on their wishes.

As a master painter and teacher, in order for my work to be remembered and pure, I needed to have no ambivalence when it came to how I saw myself. Wrapping myself in the purest white and gold Light that I could see, the world would become my personal mural. Often, I would ask myself in no uncertain terms if God had given me a gift. Always, the response was one that I knew before questioning it. Of course! But this gift did no good if I didn't treat it with the respect of life that I deemed so important for myself. This is why at every opportunity, I would invoke the power of the surreal connection to the blissful energies that the Great Creator availed to me. In my physical life, I needed to absorb the uniqueness of my soul, as well as the uniqueness of all souls. The same lesson held true for my physical body and the beauty of all bodies, regardless of shape or size. If captured in my mind in the purest of ways, then my work on the walls of life would also reflect the essence of the bouquet of beauty in all people. How extravagant I would be depended on how well I was feeling about myself on any particular day.

There were times when I would wake up just like most of you and feel discouraged about my looks, my talents, my relationships. It was during these days that my works would be more morose than they were intended to be. The gloominess would be apparent and this would put me in a dourer mood. Even the simplest of images would come out with pessimistic energies.

Other days, I would arise full of vitality, full of invigoration to face the day and all of its challenges. My paintings, all of my art forms, would take on a life of their own. Flowers would dance, the angels would appear to be singing, and the vibration from them would continue to feed my soul and resonate throughout my body. It would make me feel more perfect and fairly invincible.

The balance I needed to learn would come as I would allow myself to be touched by God. If I felt poorly, it was more important for me to reflect on the greatness of the gifts I received from the High One. Placing myself in a surrounding of His presence would lighten my thoughts and ignite, albeit slowly at times, the passion that I needed in order to succeed in what I was working on. When I felt more uplifted, my mind would simply suggest to myself that I was already connected to this Almighty Energy. Nothing would slow me down or impede my progress.

If I sound as though I were conflicted, depending upon the day, I was. The same can be said for all people. No one has ever gone through a normal physical existence and not experienced the ups and downs of mentally created moods. If you accept them as commonplace, then it is easier to deal with them on individual levels, rather than as something you feel you can't escape from for long periods of time.

It is at this point that you are being told that your reflection in the golden pond of life is directly associated with your ability to obtain and sustain a level of happiness that you want. It is also the way to intrinsically absorb the goodness of yourself and how others see you. If you think that your reflection to society isn't what you want it to be, God has given you the tools of courage and more importantly, hope. With **hope** and the bright Light guiding you, the imagery of who you are can always be substantially improved. You can carve out the insecurities and the dislikes and replace them with incredible images of things you want to reflect as to who you really are.

*   *   *   *   *   *

The acceptance of life comes more easily
when we understand that we are an energy
frequenting multiple dimensions.

*   *   *   *   *   *

I've come to notice that many times when I am personally frustrated by life and its events, someone in spirit will generally address the situation. In a variety of ways and methods, the message of hcaling comcs through. Undoubtedly, they are designed for more than myself. Most of the time, the quick story that is channeled in or the short verses lift many, many people. There was one period of time when I was reflecting on the passing of my grandfather and feeling a bit lost. At the same time, I was a magnet for people whose children passed into spirit.

Personally, this message was one of the most meaningful ones ever given to me. I hope that the following message has as much of a healing influence on you as it does for me.

*   *   *   *   *   *

IN THE LIGHT

A shadow of joy flickered; it is me. I told you I wouldn't leave. My Spirit is with you. My memories, my thoughts are imbedded deep in your heart. I still love you. Do not for one moment think you have been abandoned. I am in the Light.

In the corner, in the hall, the car, and the yard—these are the places I stay with you. My Spirit rises every time you pray for me, but my energy comes closer to you. Love does not diminish; it grows stronger. I am the feather that finds you in the yard, the balloon that dances before you, perhaps the dimmed lamp that grows brighter. In your mind, I place our memories for you to see. We lived in our special way, a way that now has its focus changed. I still crave your understanding and long for the many words of prayer and good fortune for my soul. I am in the Light.

As you struggle to adjust without me, I watch silently. Sometimes, I summon up all the strength of my new world to make you notice me. Impressed by your grief, I try to impress my love deeper into your consciousness. As you should, I call out to the heavens for help. You should know that the fountain of youth does exist. My soul is now healthy. Your love sends me newfound energy. I am adjusting to this new world. I am with you, and I am in the Light.

Please don't feel bad that you can't see me. I am with

you wherever you go. I protect you, just as you protected me so many times. Talk to me and somehow I will find a way to answer you. Mother, father, son or daughter, it makes no difference. Brother, sister, husband or wife, it makes no difference. Whatever our connection—friend or foe—I see you with my new eyes. I am learning to help wherever you are, wherever I am needed. This can be done, because I am in the Light.

When you feel despair, reach out to me. I will come. Our love for you truly does transcend from heaven to earth. Finish your life with enthusiasm and the zest that you had when we were together in the physical sense. You owe this to me, but more importantly, you owe it to yourself. Life continues for both of us. I am with you because I love you, and I am in the Light.

*   *   *   *   *   *

I've found that since I've been opened to Spirit, my ability to take things in stride when they aren't going well has improved greatly. My level of patience has grown with most people, yet for myself, the challenge continues. Life has a way of reminding me that no matter how strong a spiritual path is followed, the everyday and mundane things in the physical world still need to be dealt with. While trying to write this short section, I have been interrupted by the telephone, the dog groomer, a sales pitch, then took my niece to work and cooked dinner. What should have taken me a few minutes to do is now entering the fourth hour.

The reason I am even bothering to tell you this is that

we cannot forget to approach life with confidence. More to the point, when I was given the gift of being able to communicate with the other side, part of my thinking was that life would be so simple, and I'd be so protected from adversity that I found myself letting my guard down. It didn't take me long to realize that the life lessons, in the physical sense, still needed to be completed. If I were to succeed at anything, taking care of my "earthly" responsibilities still needed to be done.

Many of the messages I receive from Spirit allude to just that point. During one stretch of time that had me worn-out, ailing, and basically fatigued, some words of discernment came through from the Egyptian. It was a simple attempt to explain what was going on; however, as Spirit is prone to do, it was purposely cryptic. As usual, when I shared the message with other people that were in need themselves, it seemed as though the words were choreographed just for them.

At another time, One Feather also gave me one of his messages on the same subject, camouflaged as a short story or essay. For me, his words were even more powerful, as they seemed to have gone right to the core of my being. More than anything, these two messages helped me to have a broader understanding of the healing work that I was beginning to undertake. As I was having doubts about my own health, often I wondered what was supposed to be happening for the people who came to me so that I could extend healing energies to them. One of the typical outcomes of these channeled lessons is that on a subconscious level, they become ingrained in me. When I work with different people, invariably, some of the words will come out of my mouth "voluntarily" while I stay tuned into what is needed.

This next message was given to me in 1996. The only reason I am giving you this information is that the same message was given to me almost verbatim ten years later. In fact, I thought I was having another memory lapse in the timing of it. Often, my soul is transported back in time in order for Spirit to solidify their message. Sometimes, this will leave me feeling the same message has been duplicated when it really hasn't been. In this particular case, it was repeated.

THE EGYPTIAN—

Sometimes in life we are given challenges. They may seem unfair, especially if you have lived a life of goodwill and proper thinking. God has not given any individual on earth the complete plan to the Kingdom of Mankind. Being such, you may never know why you must endure situations that seem to epitomize the exact opposite of what we are striving to accomplish.

You have been given one such challenge. It is an obstacle that tempts you to throw away your faith in a Higher Power, yet, it should be seen by you as a further way to prove your love, admiration, and respect for the Supreme Being. Perhaps it is a show of respect for what you have proved in this lifetime. The biggest burdens are given to the people who have the ability to trust, pray, and believe that they will overcome all blockages on their way to the Great Kingdom.

147

As a child of Spirit, a piece of Him lives within. You must remember this so that you can firmly believe that all forms of illnesses and fatigue to the body are fully capable of being overcome. Every single human is given more than a chance to produce affirmative results when the physical body ails. The ever-present, all-powerful mind and soul is what controls your cadence. Stepping through the challenge you are now faced with can come easier with the admittance that there is a situation that has to be reckoned with and by showing Spirit the serious intent in which you are willing to beat back the obstacle.

Progression and participation in your own healing is what is most mandatory within the realm of awareness. Keeping your thoughts positive and your consciousness to a higher level enables God and Spirit to come to your aid. Love yourself enough to want to save the goodness and grace of humanity that you represent. Remembering that life is a gift and loaned to the soul for growth should give you a sense of urgency. Be urgent only in your quest to maintain the strong foundation you have set in motion.

The legacy of your life should never be forgotten, especially by you. Be proud and procure the inducement of Love and Light from all of God's Kingdom. You are being given a chance to taste victory, to taste the rewards of being you. Blessings come to all who ask and all who earn them. Request assistance and you will be carried as long as you find it in your heart to resist the temptation of negativity. You are never alone, and alone you must never feel.

*   *   *   *   *   *

ONE FEATHER—
THE HEALER

There was the cry of an eagle being heard as it circled above. Upon looking up, I realized how free it was. Unattached by any physical plight, the bird flew almost motionlessly, a glory and confidence abounded as it felt its own safety from his Master. Freedom. More freedom. The question was asked, "How is it that my own illness traps me when there is so much to see?"

With that question in mind, a voice told me that I, too, could be free. I was confused and perplexed by this thought. How could I be free in my condition? Again, I heard the same voice tell me that I could be released from my constraints. I sat on the ground and looked up again at the magnificent bird that seemed to be at harmony with its surroundings.

"How could I be like that bird? There aren't any burdens being placed on him." I spoke these words, but to whom they were directed, I did not know.

Disoriented because of these thoughts, I took another glance at the eagle and with all my strength, moved from within range. I was crippled by the limitations to my physical body. I scoffed at the notion I could be free. Suddenly, my thoughts went to an acquaintance I met in the hospital. He was doing much better than I, and it appeared to me that his recovery was aided by some mystical power. Truly, that isn't something that could happen to me, or could it? I glowered at the notion and continued my painful movement back to my room.

Now, thoroughly depressed, I reached the door. Something kept me from entering into the darkness. It became dark outside where I was now, and from within, I could see brightness. Fear paralyzed me. I had no concept of what was occurring. My hand moved ahead, and I unlocked the door, and with trepidation, stepped into the light. To my surprise, the eagle I had been looking at was calmly perched in front of me.

My child," he said, "why is it that you think you are unworthy to be healed?"

I responded by telling him that the outside world turned its back on me, that I was no longer able to seek comfort for my condition from anyone.

"This comfort you seek is in yourself. If you want to feel loved, you must begin by not feeling confined. There is a world waiting for you, a world so powerful that to ignore it means your own demise. From within the mind of man, God gave you the power to overcome all hardships. Leave the crippled feeling behind. Simply, all you must do is believe. The mystical power is there for everyone."

These words seemed so ordinary, but the eagle reassured me that my destiny was controlled only by myself. I heeded his wisdom and thankfully expressed my gratitude. As I did this, the door flew open, the eagle left, and I now knew that I was the one who could soar. I was free.

*   *   *   *   *   *

A harrowing experience when given over to the universe becomes a halo experience. Let the angels guide you to triumphant paths.

*   *   *   *   *   *

The grace of God is simply the Light, Life, and Love He entrusts and bestows upon you.

*   *   *   *   *   *

Somebody asked me once how I knew that God and Spirit were around us. It was a question that's been asked of me many times, and through my lips would come a host of different connections. One deeper, more thought-provoking message was given to me by One Feather, who always seems to have the right words for the right person. Initially, I wasn't sure if I understood it, but it all makes more sense after it is reread a few times. Many of his messages seem to contain variable interpretations, even though you may think you are reading or hearing it the same way each time. This was one of them.

ONE FEATHER—
REFLECTION

I stood in a puddle of water and watched it as the rain turned it into a lake. There was a feeling of distress as I saw an old friend. Once tall and proud, now standing alone, tired, and worn. Time went by and the rain continued to fall. My friend was solemn, sad, and wrought with anxiety and pain. The skies darkened, the birds, the animals were silent. My friend began to wither as the air around him became dark and dank. Total despair.

A sparkle of light, a feather came before him. A hand reached out in a loving way, but my friend—now confused—reneged in grasping it. With patience of time behind it, the hand moved closer. My friend now weakly allowed himsclf to be pulled from his knees. Again on his feet, he allowed himself to be embraced. The rain stopped, birds began to sing, the water receded. Flowers began to grow. The sky became light.

I heard a voice say, "With me you are, with you I am."

At that moment, I realized the darkness was my fear, the sadness was my plight. The rains were tears—my own tears. The hand that was given to me came from God. Finally, I understood the embrace was the love of life instilled by the power of the energy that was always there. My friend once again stood tall and in a flash, I knew **he was me.**

*   *   *   *   *   *

Have you ever said to yourself, "I wish I could just be happy," or "What will it take to make me happy?" These are normal thoughts and ones that hop into my mind a lot more than I'd like to admit. I was having these same queries on one particularly rough, emotional day. As usual, Spirit showed me that there is not a single time when there is no one around to listen.

A voice started booming in my head, one that I was unfamiliar with. Visually, he looked like an ancient Chinese man with a long, scraggly beard and wispy mustache. He was in a lotus sitting position, and I could see him usher me to take a seat in front of him as though he were ready to play the role of the teacher. Learning not to fight this tug at my soul and self, I allowed myself to go into a light meditative trance to hear what he had to say.

THE TEACHER—

My child, happiness is not something that you have to work at. Happiness is built into the soul. If you were having a lifetime of hardships, where you never had a joyous occasion or uplifting view of something taking place, then I could understand your dilemma. The truth is that all people encounter a level of happiness in some form.

No one has gone through life without ever giving a smile to someone or even to themselves when they witness something that brings that simple gesture to their lips. It is a form of being happy. Have you ever laughed at a joke, a funny situation? This is happiness. Have you ever taken a long walk or a ride somewhere and thought about how beautiful the scenery is? Did you get a good feeling? This is happiness.

Have you ever felt the joy of holding a newborn? How about the glee from watching the antics of a playful puppy or kitten? Does a golden sunset make you recognize its beauty? Do you remember the ecstasy you may have felt when you were a teenager and had a heart-throbbing attraction to someone? The reason I bring these few examples up are because you don't have to find happiness—happiness is already part of you.

When the Shambala Master created Earth, He did so with the emotions of joy, love, sadness, confidence, esteem, and much more. Your emotions are not something that need to be found. They are built in. There is no truth to the fact that you have to find how to be happy; rather, it is up to you to recall it. Remember the times in your lives where you felt uplifted and free? Remember the euphoric feelings of finding a special piece of candy as a child, or perhaps the romance and intense passion you felt with a soul that is an equal to who you are? I ask you, do you have to figure out how to be happy when a windfall comes to you?

These are emotions that need to be stirred up. It is your right not to dwell on what makes you smile, but it is more of a right to do just that. Embrace the succulently sweet energies of your life, of yourself. Allow the significance of elation to blend into your everyday thoughts—and don't fight it. It is a gift from God for you to be enthralled with who you are and an inborn right for you to recall happiness at all times, even in the times of dismay. All of our children [an image given of all people] are important to those of us in the Kingdom of Light. How silly it would be for you to have to learn what it is like to be happy when happiness is surrounding you. It is one of those subjects that will have you overcomplicating the nature of its intent. Just as the God Being is all around and ever-present, so, too, is your choice to be happy.

If I've made myself clear, then the progress of your soul and self should understand that by processing life a little differently, searching for the feeling of happiness doesn't have to be anything more than a mental adjustment. Virtual anticipation of pleasantries in life is vital to the sense of contentment that you seek. A wise man once told me that the intent of your attitude overrides the outcome of all of life's operations, both good and bad. What he meant by this was that you alone, with strong and positively placed thoughts and ideas, can overcome all feelings of sadness, anger, frustrations, and futility. Be happy. Be proud. Be strong in your attempts to feel the euphoria of energies. After all, your life is grounded only by the heaviness of your thoughts.

With all that said, can you see the future plate of satisfaction? Can you see the smile on your lips that is alive, although maybe aloof, in yourself? Bring to light the awareness of the mutual sense of self-worth when you amass the greatest and deepest powers of available joy. It is yours to feel, to save, and to share at all times, but mostly it should be freely shared with the importance of yourself.

*   *   *   *   *   *

You live in heaven and you live in hell when you are in a life on earth. This is what we are trying to get you to understand. Heaven, and the wonderment and beauty of it, is already available for you, but through all past teachings, from a human standpoint, it is unknown and unclear. This is why we want for the new movement to teach of the power and love that comes from positive affirmations and beliefs. If you are truly happy living on earth, then the afterlife, which is more impressive, would not have to be looked at as a relief from your incarnation, but rather as an extension to greater things.

*   *   *   *   *   *

How do we trust what we can't see? Just as you trust there is air to breathe, Spirit is also wrapped around you.

*   *   *   *   *   *

Over the years, those in spirit have sent many strong messages through to me so that people can understand that the influence created by their own actions is tantamount to success. Frequently, I hear about the Law of the Universe and the Law of Prosperity. As often happens to me, it is seldom that I consciously remember any part of the channeled messages until I read back the transcript or listen to whatever may have been recorded. During my attempts to put the right passages together for this book, I came across the words that follow. It was one of the earlier messages sent to me and one that until now, I forgot even came through. Hopefully, it will have the depth of importance to each of you that it was intended to have.

THE INFLUENCE OF WORDS

Make the most of your thoughts, ideas, and concerns. You must remember that the suggested meaning of what runs through your mind can register results equally, whether it is positive or negative. Understand the following guidelines to ensure that you make life what you want with your words.

If you have the ability to see, then watch the havoc or happiness your words can create.

If you have the ability to hear, then listen to the message you are sending while you speak.

If you have a heart, then you have the ability to feel the words that are spoken.

Understand these three principles and you have the foundation to accept responsibility for all your words—good or bad. With this knowledge and that of the Law of Return, you are able to engage your existence in a most joyful light. Keep in mind that everyone has the same rights. Doesn't it make sense, then, for happiness, love, and prosperity to come to all of mankind?

*　　*　　*　　*　　*　　*

Spiritual abundance is like a large, permanent waterfall. You may never completely understand the volume, yet it always finds a way to be replenished. Small trickles can grow into powerful forces.

*   *   *   *   *   *

Have you ever quietly sat somewhere, simply trying to put the day behind you? Maybe some of the frustrations surfaced more than they needed to, or perhaps you were just a bit agitated by one issue and let it carry over into others. Our emotions are the way in which we cope with life. That simple fact is not something that I really ever dwelled on, but those in spirit have a way of making you understand the infinite interconnections to God.

On one fairly lonely night, I was sitting at the computer trying to think of how I could motivate myself to get more done. Thoughts of companionship and love seemed to dance through my mind. All of the aches and pains in my body became intensified, and a growing agitation was taking over. Many times, this is how Spirit will "retrieve" me so that they can impart an idea or much more. Most of the time, I don't mind, but every now and then, all I want to do is live a life that is free of this responsibility—and truthfully, at times—a bother. Usually, that is when my friends on the other side become more relentless in their pursuit of my time and attention. One night, I was compelled to listen more closely than I cared to, not that I didn't want to, but because my eyelids were already heavy and the last thing I desired to do was channel by virtue of taping or typing. This is what I heard and understood much better well after the fact.

YO TSANG TSU—

Listen to me, my child. I have come with nothing but good intentions and a message of symbolic power for all to hear. To begin, you must agree to the fact and foundation of union with the Shambala Energies. What this means is that even though you may feel isolated and alone, the presence of God is with you. This allows you to feel a revitalized approach to life.

The way to get this to work for you is to simply sit quietly, quell your thoughts, and focus on the goals you want to achieve. Keep in mind that these goals must be realistic in the realm of your life as it is in the moment; however, thinking about **improving** on it is acceptable. Gentle music playing in the background can be helpful, and if you can listen to some with the melodic sounds of nature, you will find it even easier to feel cupped by the energy of the Highest One.

As you practice letting go of the stresses in your life, what will be invoked is the contentment of inner peace. Perhaps you will feel a vibration of energy similar to a buzzing or the flutter of a flying insect in the palm of your hand when you cup it with love. It may feel like the beginning of what you see as "goose bumps," but I assure you, it is the strength of the softest, yet most powerful source of Light and inspiration in the universe.

This is what it first feels like when you touch the outer edge of the presence of your God. It is also something that you can learn to do in a deeper, more profound assimilation with Him. By relaxing your mind, the integration you desire to have with the deepest aspect of

159

the Golden Side will become more readily available as you learn to trust the connection. It is of extreme urgency that you allow this bond and union to flourish.

Try not to let your intellectual mind determine what you are feeling. As soon as you do that, the simplicity and ease of union between the physical and esoteric worlds becomes compromised. One of the things you will look for is the sense of a golden hue and calmer assent in the way your mind reacts to this slowed down pattern of thinking. This is the way you start to release the agitation and blockages to a path of serenity.

You can also use soothing aromas to help heighten the physical pleasantries that your brain is capable of producing. My children, you will find it helpful to have an odor of ginger, lavender, or other relaxing scents. Sometimes you might feel that it helps if you can re-create aromas that return your mind to very happy and fond remembrances from your childhood or anytime in the past. The release of the chemicals within your brain will help you to build on a foundation of excitement. At the same time, it is simply helping you to feel eased about your frustrations so that you can begin to see the pattern of production and motivation that you want to obtain for yourself.

Once you have mastered this capability, it then becomes your job not to let the negatives of life, or the negativity of the people around you, demean the approach to carving a new niche in the reality you are striving to make. The mantra you must repeat in a consistent manner is, "I am, I will, and I can be the person I desire to be. This is because my God is with me and in me. No one can stop me from being productive and happy."

Repeating positive mantras are valuable in retraining your brain to think in that manner. In actuality, you are converting your subconscious thoughts to become more effective in molding your daily actions to be more productive. If you are productive, then the aspirations to feel more motivated to conquer your own problems are much easier. Life's frustrations become less intense and begin to become spaced further and further from each episode. We create our reality through the conscious declaration of our thoughts. The vast ease and simplicity that life can be for us, for all of God's children, comes from the labeling of ideas.

The topic has now turned towards positive or negative affirmations concerning **everything** in life. If you have an injury or malady and expect pain to be the outcome, then you are in pain. Consider those who have broken a bone. The initial physical feeling is intense and sometimes excruciating pain. This persists until you are under the thought, or possibly the illusion, that help is about to be given. All of a sudden, the anguish you felt only moments before begins to diminish. You have invoked an attitude of "This will be alright," and by doing so, you found a way to have a lot of the discomfort abate. The concept here falls under the Law of Attraction.

What would happen if the same problem occurred and you did not expect pain? To a great degree, the mind would override the physical chaos and the problem wouldn't be so drastic. Have you ever wondered why some people can do so well in a time of crisis and others panic? The same aspects of what I've mentioned must take hold of their desires and future plans. It is here that I reaffirm to you that you have the drive to accomplish anything you wish to finish. And that, my children, is the key. You must want to finish what is started, as well as finish what has not yet started.

Imagine now that if what you are able to create with your own consciousness, for your own personal changes, could also be used to make changes in your environment. This is simple logic. If you have the ability to produce positive outcomes by allowing your thoughts to vibrate at a higher, more efficient level, then there is nothing in the realm of this universe that cannot be affected by the approach you take. Think about how good it feels to jump-start yourself and all things around you. Why wouldn't you work on the simple task of deflating your ego and instead, inflate with the love and positive intellect and force of the Master of Light?

Of course, I have just made this sound like an easy thing to do. It is! The reality is that it does take practice. You should not feel ashamed about an inability to do this the first time you try, but it is well within the range of conceptual alliance. In other words, if you trust that you can conceive and understand the vivid and bright outcome beforehand, then you have the power to embrace your ability to consciously submit to happiness, love, romance, optimism, usefulness, and oneness with God. Perhaps the first thing you should tell yourself is that if you have trouble in easing the load of dreariness and depression that are keeping you from accomplishing great feats, that you will accept and embrace the opportunity to try repeatedly. Eventually, you will incorporate it into the center of your personal universe, that being the God within.

* * * * * *

When our hearts are anchored to the wisdom and wishes of Spirit, our souls will soar.

* * * * * *

Pain is relevant only if the mind allows it.

* * * * * *

The power of healing through mind clearance and visualization cannot be underscored enough.

* * * * * *

If there has been one aspect that Spirit has made me familiar with, it is the fact that we are expected to make mistakes. The hope is that we learn from them and formulate the changes so we can grow as a person. It is not unfamiliar to have those in spirit repeat the same lesson over and over, throughout the years. By doing this, we are being taught that no one is expected to be as perfect as we think we need to be. Constant reminders are sent through the lessons so that we can see that who we are is God, but being His energy does not mean that we need to be perfect in the physical sense. It is up to us to learn how to achieve the quality in our life that we deem necessary for our survival and success.

One of my main interests, since the inception of my awareness of the communication I was having with Spirit, was my involvement with healing people. It kept me up many nights because I'd allow my mind to wander and dream about having a profound and positive impact on as many people as possible. The other reason I would be awake at night would come from all the patterns of symbols and healing energies that would float around my physical and psychic eye. Most of the time, I still have no conscious ability to be able to translate, or interpret, what I'm seeing, but my subconscious mind has been absorbing these nonsensical geometric configurations into some form of internal intelligence.

Basically, the origin of healing goes back thousands of years. This is what written communiqués tell us. There are many stories of great healers, such as Buddha and Jesus, helping individuals overcome illnesses that at that time seemed to be incurable. What Spirit has shown me is that our bodies can create physical changes by virtue of mental belief that we will be healed. Today, stories of this sort should be written over and over again; however, the mass population is in a state of needing everything to be visually or scientifically proved. This causes a dilemma in the fact that we don't believe as freely as in past centuries, thereby limiting the true reconstruction abilities that the body/mind connection has.

Many of the personal messages I receive from Spirit are about the body's resiliency and the power of the mind in reducing pain. This reduction process started many years ago, well before I was opened to my spiritual path. At times, it has caused problems for me and this is where I want to personally caution you. If you are going to attempt to control your mind into limiting health issues, you have to be certain to fully and consciously acknowledge the other areas it might be affecting. Being able to withstand pain is counterproductive if you are not following through on "seeing" the cure for what ails you. Otherwise, you might be reducing the pain, but allowing the problem to flourish.

The following is most of the transcript from a prayer and meditation meeting held more than ten years ago. It basically puts into focus what I've been writing about and is worth remembering.

EGYPTIAN—

I wish to speak to all of you about the subject of health. In this room tonight, many different forms of energy were felt. Some felt it as heat, some felt it as wind, others spun, and some felt depressed. Still, there were other sensations not easily explained in human terms. All of these energies were given tonight so that we could further show each of you the variations and the power in which all people can be healed.

Sometimes discomfort must take place before permanent rectification and purification of the physical body is had. In the minds of all men are the strength and the wisdom to focus and guide you to a better way of life.

You must all understand that the healing process comes not only from the medical world, but more so from the spiritual realm. Situations, not only in this room but in all the world, are seen as evidence that the workings of God and Spirit make for unusual happenings and positive results. Just as purification of the airways is necessary, purification of the mind must also be prominent. We hope to inspire you to review the thoughts that you let seep out of your mind. These thoughts are what generate positive or negative results in all physical, emotional, or mental conditions.

Tumors are being reduced as we sit here tonight. Eradication of these growths is being sped up. A cyclone of energy is directed at the center of the problem. Understand that each of you who develop physical ailments do not develop them for yourself. See them as being Spirit's problems and release them to the universe. This is a great departure from ordinary thinking. Pharmaceutical products have been created not only scientifically for your benefit, but have been created naturally thousands and thousands of years ago for use in all systems. In your lifetime, you will hear of diseases being dismissed as only a dysfunction for a minor problem, rather than life threatening as they are now. You have to look no further back then at the creation of the dissolution of polio. Only those ignorant of the vaccine will have the chance to be stricken by this, but even the chance of coming down with such a harmful disease is greatly lessened as the number of carriers have dwindled so greatly. The same holds true for other diseases that have been virtually removed from the natural process of survival.

Emotional gains come not only through your prayers, but also through assistance from your friends and family. It is important for all of you to understand and to know that many people are only seconds away, either by use of the phone, the car, or simply by walking to them. I point this out so that you can be aware that no battle in anyone's life has to be undergone secretively and in a world full of loneliness. If you do not reach forward, the message you send is that you do not deem yourself worthy of repair. An expression of yours is that "the squeaky wheel gets the oil." We would like all of you to squeak to Spirit and to squeak to your friends so that the oil of love and life can be spread upon you.

Never be afraid to take someone's hand and ask for assistance. This is the most important part of the message tonight. Healings come when you readily ask for help from others. Whether you pray openly to Spirit or you talk freely to your friends, it does not matter. The results will be positive because positive thoughts will be given to you.

When was the last time you heard of somebody being overrun by a harmful disease and being put down or given negative directives by their friends when they were approached? A common trigger for all humans is a **humanitarian outlook** and one **to give hope** to everyone. This is why it is so important for you to understand that serenity and happiness are at your fingertips.

Investigate the use of natural substances. In this world, there is an item or a counterbalance for every ailment. Different plants create different sensations. Some are used to stimulate the mind, others are used to purify the blood, and some are used as energy enhancers. These are the ones we would like you to look at. As you keep your energy levels high, you keep your spiritual body spinning. With this spin, it is difficult for negativity to attach itself. This is because all bad or so-called evil thoughts move at a slower vibration. The vibration of life is what we need for all of you to see. Visualizations of your own happiness and your own perfect health will lead just to that.

*   *   *   *   *   *

As I sat at the computer and wondered whether or not this book was close to coming to a conclusion, Spirit bellowed to me that it is not about a beginning or an end. It is about living to the best of our abilities. Life is about freedom of the heart, mind, body, and lessons for the soul.

There are no coincidences in our physical life. The longer I work with and through Spirit, the more I recognize that we are given what we need at a particular time. Recently, I was in a bookstore where my personal mission was to find a book I had been told about to give as a gift. Instead of going to the sports section of literature, I was drawn to browse in a completely different area. It was while I was absent-mindedly glancing at different titles that I heard someone call my name.

When I turned to see who it was, my eyes focused on

Jay Sears, the founder of The Mission of Kindness. Jay has an energy and bright aura and does exceptional work with the homeless, the addicted, and the needy. He pays great attention to the children of the world and gives selflessly to help as many people as he can. Jay recanted several anecdotal stories about his mission, and I felt strangely diminished by his efforts.

While I have been thinking that I am doing everything I can and am abiding by Spirit's wishes, Jay made me spend the rest of the day reflecting on what more can be done to spread happiness, as well as love to the world. He also made me feel like I haven't even begun to touch the mass population with the inspiration that we can all have from living in the spiritual zone. Referring to a life of good intentions never entered my mind as "a zone" until I was educated by Jay's words. The funny thing is that I don't think he even knew he was impacting me so strongly on this day. Jay and I had seen each other several times over the last few years, but for some reason, Spirit wanted me to be redirected in what I am supposed to be doing.

This brings me back to something that was previously mentioned. It is not always very easy for us to adhere to the requests of Spirit because we are so often looking at life and what they want from us in a monolithic aspect. This makes us naturally fear doing almost anything that we are unfamiliar with. More so, when we don't understand the intent of a message from the other side, we tend to dig our heels in and not proceed with it. We need to learn to trust in the fact that if we follow their instructions, we will be brought to a higher place in our daily existence.

Much of what I refer to now is the desire for all of us to be encouraged to direct ourselves in such a way that we can feel as if we were relieved of a gigantic burden. How many times have you wondered what it was going to take to finally be happy? In my case, it is a question that might seem rhetorical, but I am well aware of the responses I get from Spirit. All people have this innate ability to connect to God and Spirit without realizing it because our voices and thoughts are heard even when we didn't think or intend for them to be listened to.

While I am writing this, the year is nearing an end. It is a time where most people reflect on the accomplishments over the last twelve months. Sometimes it is about remembering loved ones we've lost in the physical world. It is, and should also be, a time when we visualize or set new goals for the coming year. That was the point I was at when I heard the following passage.

*   *   *   *   *   *

UNKNOWN SPIRIT—

God has granted all people a year of adjustments. He has set forth a new and rigorous desire for all of His children to arise and greet the challenges of the New Year with an invigoration beyond any they have felt before. Are you ready to ride the crest of the wave of inspiration, success, love, spirituality, hope, and completion? Do not choose to ignore the bounties of opportunities that are coming! Behold the Christ consciousness!

It is now up to all of you to omnipotently ban together to revile those who try to remove God and all Higher Presence from everyday life. As an individual, hidden from the fallacies of fanfare, you must use every capability you have to allow your voice to echo amongst those He chooses to reform life on the behalf of those who have no clue. Let your words reverberate to lawmakers and tax collectors, schools and organizations that have chosen to ill-advisedly try to scourge the love of God in order to appease the misinformed and spiritually misaligned. The world and this country were created with the premise of peace and love, as well as the tenets of the facets of the Ten Commandments. This was done to insure that even though evil-minded men and women continue to walk the plains of the earth, their voices will not drown out the vibrant and God-believing souls who infuse their neighborhoods with blessed harmony.

You must see this as the year to reclaim love and to pour through the values of peaceful harmony amongst the physical and the spiritual. Rise above the dissatisfaction and diminutive thoughts of those whose agenda is self-serving. Take the time to reseat your goals and dreams so that no one can take away anything you want. Let rise up all those who are of good intentions and help sink those who do not want to abide by the Laws of the Universe.

On a more personal note, arrange all things that you want to do so that a plan of intelligent attack can be formulated. List out everything you'd like to do, regardless of how far-fetched you may feel the thought is. By first putting things in print, you already are paving the way for the manifestation of lights to lead you onto the path of joy. Organize your list into the need and balance for true importance. Never erase those things that come to mind initially, for even if the physical world may not be ready to give them to you, the spiritual world will begin to process it for the right timing.

Imbibe yourself with the Love and Light of God! Center your thoughts to the manifestation of greatness, no matter how small or inconsequential you may currently feel. In the eyes of God and Spirit, you are never overlooked or deemed unimportant. Make sure you see yourself as being able to physically enjoy the arena that is your existence. Take care of your body, as well as your mind and soul.

Finally, you should, and will, begin to enhance your understanding of the importance of tithing to spiritually promoting groups, causes, and the like. By understanding the scheme of prosperity, all tithes, when given from the heart, will lead to the abundance and abilities you need to further yourselves. God will see to this throughout your physical life. Accept it, embrace it, and share it. May the peace and tranquility you have always wanted fall gracefully into your aura.

*   *   *   *   *   *

Evil temptation is the crack in the foundation of the soul.

*   *   *   *   *   *

*Performance can be the mirror image of what
we had been
thinking we wanted to do. How well do you perform?*

*   *   *   *   *   *

The days seem to fly by for me since Spirit chose to allow me to connect with them. Of course, they tell me it's that I allowed myself to do the connecting. Nevertheless, the passion I have for God and Spirit grows internally each day. This comes with a flurry of constant questions, such as, **"Why isn't life easier for us to get through?"**

Recalling how many times I go through my day feeling off balance, insecure, and unsure of myself is impossible for me to relay to anyone. Time and again, depression and happiness oppose each other, seemingly from one minute to the next. It is a true challenge for me to stay on top of what *I know* I'm supposed to do according to the messages I get for myself. This has to be balanced with the more obstinate opposition I give Spirit because I either don't like what is being told to me or flat-out don't feel comfortable or confident enough in myself to achieve it. During these times, my rebalancing comes when I take a step back or just simply give myself a breather from the daily grind. It is supposed to be that way for all of you as well.

As this newest year approaches, while I extend the words and passages of this book, I find myself in need of such a break, however, there seems to be an unknown excitement about what will be happening in the next twelve months and beyond. The anticipation I feel is one that is making me literally very nervous, but the sense of impending change is something that Spirit tells me will help me, my family and friends, and then a mass of others as I trust in the Light that leads me. Even now, while I'm writing this and heard Spirit say, "The masses will be encouraged by your expression of words and works," only adds to what I still want to see as my inability to honor them in the way they want me to.

I have often marveled at the variety of ways and approaches that Spirit seems to be able to open our eyes to their existence. Sometimes it is as simple as a thought that pops in our mind unexpectedly. Other times, you could be looking at the cloud formation and see in them a clear image of an animal or any other of a multitude of items.

This Christmas Eve, I felt compelled to return to my religious roots. For the first time since before I opened to Spirit, I felt a need to attend midnight mass. There is always a reason for these things, whether you can, or want to, understand it or not. Sometimes, Spirit will find a way to make even the staunchest of disbelievers comprehend the validity and realness of God. Sometimes, for someone like myself, a little gift of reassurance that there is indeed a Higher Energy other than what we feel on earth makes me feel better. Anyway, when I pulled into my driveway and got out of the car at about 1:20 AM, I saw what I surmised was a shooting star. It looked like a streak of light dashing before me, but was mesmerizing to me for other reasons that I only knew about spiritually. It was my gift. Even though I lived on the water for a couple of years and had great views of the night skyline, this was the first time I witnessed this cosmic event. For some people, that is all it would be seen as, a cosmic event. For me, it was what I had been longing to see and never had the privilege of. For a moment, I could *feel* God. That isn't new for me, but it is mostly unspoken.

Another "thought" was just given to me. It is up to us, as individuals, to feel comfortable with our concepts of who God is and what Spirit and spirituality is all about. Even though all the varieties of proper religions have their basis of beliefs, God is a personal asset and aspect. For me, even though I don't attend regular church services nearly as much as I was brought up to believe I should, my connection with God is much greater every day that I'm given the opportunity to start fresh. Regardless of what goes wrong in my life, somehow I can always pull myself towards the image that I am not enduring all of the disruptions alone. It is a form of blind faith and not anything I have ever received from any of the mainstream churches I've attended over the years.

This is the same faith that makes us have hope for our future. It is something that has always intrigued me and what led me to meditate on the question of what or why is it that we deem it necessary to see the future in bright tones and ignore much of what is wrong in our lives today. The following is what Spirit enabled me to channel.

*   *   *   *   *   *

UNKNOWN SPIRIT—

My son, it is you who needs to be embellished with the searing joys of happiness. Why is it that you feel it important to rely on the negatives of the world? Have you lost your way? Are you intentionally staying lost in the ways of your parents, the ways of all old teachings? Don't you want to forge a path of newness, a path of success, peace, happiness, and contentment? It is not demeaning to want enlightened awareness. All people are entitled to it.

By looking towards the future with a scintilla of hope, all that which is bad in life then becomes bearable. God wants you to be happy. God wants you to be able to absorb new ideas, even if that means you have to create a new identity in how you approach life and its entire splendor. People should not be afraid to rewrite negative perceptions of what life might be about. Most often, these thoughts and teachings have come from your parents and other participants in molding your outlook. Have you ever taken the time to really and truly analyze why you act, think, or perceive an issue to be what you believe? Can you tell if it comes from your own mind, or are the basic fundamentals coming from something you were taught and blindly obeyed or followed?

Peering at the future with a sense of euphoria is God-given. It is His thought and hope that you, your friends, and their families all seek this glory. God and Spirit are not about to have you look at the days ahead with a wretched forbearing, with angst, animosity, and distrust. Those are all man-created concepts. All He wants is for you to soar to the greatest peaks of the world, to dare to view life as a physical feat that is worthy of embracing. It is this type of light that should be shining in your mind, not a light that is dim and shadowy.

Why do you fear a future of happiness? What is it that makes you think that if you are processing negative things, that when they happen, you won't be unprepared or hurt? You will still be feeling the emotional and mental frustrations!

Let us prepare to teach each of you about changing your perceptions. Are you ready for some of the simplest information we can give you from Spirit? First, you must understand that you need to reformat your ingrained childhood teachings. What do we mean by this? It's simple. All people are taught a series of "dos and don'ts" when growing up. It is from this foundation that your adult decisions and life is transcended. Everything you do going forward is based upon the belief concepts that you were taught.

From today, we ask that you disregard most of the common thoughts about why negatives and a feeling of lack are all right. You will begin to consciously make a list of all things you have heard that are untrue, such as something as simple as, "Money can't buy happiness," or "Money is the root of all evil." Now, we are not specifically targeting finances here. We are using it so that on a basic level, you can clearly acknowledge how these, as well as conversations about health, love, romance, and so on, are often followed simply because we blindly absorb what is supposed to be factual information. Do I have your attention?

I [Spirit] want to know if we have your attention so that we can reposition your philosophies simply by making you write down how many clichés you have heard about from all topics in life that don't make sense. If the thought is negative, write it down. Review the list, then dispose of it when you are confident you have remembered them all. By taking this action, you are symbolically telling the universe that you are ready for something better for yourself, now and forever forward.

After accomplishing the symbolism of removing the negative memory system in you, take time to establish new, positive, uplifting goals and thoughts. Write them down legibly and continue to add to this list as new thoughts emerge daily. Make sure you put this new, vibrant product in a place that can easily be seen and read.

If it helps, place your goals in sections or by category. For some people, it is helpful to focus on finances, romance, health, and overall wellness. You can have a list for social goals, for educational goals, and more. In fact, you can have as many different goal lists as you want as long as you take the time to read, absorb, and act on them. Without any hesitation, we will bring to you all those items that are of proper quality and conceptually sound in the aspects that will help your future reshape itself towards the positive progression you desire. Keep in mind that ***progression through action*** is the catalyst for life's happiness. The only question to you, or anyone, is this: "Do you really want to be happy, or is it something that you feel is too far beyond your grasp?"

If you want to seize happiness, then start now!

Procrastination only averts the beginning stages of what you are looking for. Be fearless about beginning, even if you sense a little edginess or apprehension. These are normal human feelings and should not be seen as a sign of anything deeper. Trust that the gift you are looking for is worthy of being yours. Get excited! Get motivated!

*   *   *   *   *   *

Suffice it to say that after channeling and reading it back to myself, I felt somewhat under-whelmed by my own thoughts. This is nothing new to me since the ability to communicate with Spirit came to the forefront. Amazingly, I am still not able to adhere to all of the suggestions and lessons that are often given to me or sent through me. Spirit tells me that this is because I'm human.

That brings me to say to all of you that it is the patience of the Higher Side that allows us to make mistakes over and over again. There seems to be an unspoken doctrine in spirit that enables us to strive to be better, yet if we fail, the love, respect, and admiration for each of us has not been revoked. I've learned that the real problem is whether or not we are ready to admit that our thoughts are worthy, or unworthy, as an individual. It is mostly from this emotion and idea that we acknowledge truth and awareness in our interpretations of God and all Higher Powers.

We must all look at the causes for how we think. Was it something that you unwittingly worked at, or is it more true to say that our feelings are not emancipated from the teachings of pertinent family and friends? Through the years, including the current one, I am always being guided towards expanding changes within my life and myself. I have been made completely aware of the vitality needed to be successful, yet some of the many thoughts and goals created from Spirit for myself do not always sit well inside me. All this means is that for me, on a personal level, I know that my connection to God is still evolving. It reminds me of the many instances where clients have sat before me and felt like they were given a reprieve by a passed-over loved one when informed that they should be fearless in moving themselves forward in their lives.

This fact is not lost on my spiritual journey. Being encouraged to release ourselves from negative escapades, from negative teachings, only enables us to grow more and more as an individual. Many on the other side of the energy realm cherish this individuality. They show through signs, some subtle and some more direct, that we can, and should, inflate our minds to reach to the deepest points and our most advanced intellectual goals. Some of what you sense you may need to do will go in direct contrast to what you want to do. This is the way of Spirit. The only agenda they have is for all people to be loved, happy, and to succeed in whatever we deem important.

An area of interest that has been brought up previously is one of financial aspects. Most of my life, thoughts of wealth and positive success were always a focus. The unfortunate thing is that I based a lot of my actions on the fact that I should only expect to survive; that to be wealthy would mean that I'd be going against some invisible law that said you have to be doing something wrong or illegal. In the earliest messages given to me from Spirit, they completely contradicted that concept.

Even as I sit at the keyboard now, impressions of success are flashing before my mind's eye. It is a consistent reminder that we are all supposed to cherish the infinite abundance that is mandated by the Law of the Universe. This means that no one should have to struggle, but people do because of misinformed family, friends and a society that teach us not to expect to receive. It is something they learned and passed along. The message that is always drummed into me, as it should be to you, is one of acceptance. All of life is a balance. There is a taker for every giver, just as there is something to balance every action in nature.

How many times have you had something offered to you and turned it down? For some reason we find it easier to say "no thank you" instead of simply, "thank you." By nature, we are generally giving people. The conflict with that is that there has to be a recipient. Somehow, many of us get that confused feeling, like we are being needy or taking advantage of something. Ironically, that is what Spirit wants us to do—take advantage of the offers of giving. However, bear in mind that it is expected that you will also do some giving. If you fall into any financial windfall, it is wise to tithe at least ten percent to spiritually promoting causes, to groups that utilize it for the continued goodwill of both man and nature. This, in turn, will allow more and more pathways to be opened to you for successful opportunities throughout your life.

A valued lesson learned from this is that we are all seen and treated equally by those on the Higher Side. If we could, as humans, reign in even half of this fundamental outlook, then peace throughout the world would not be an issue. As that sentence was typed, Spirit told me, "That message will be seen by those who refuse to understand their role in society as being a Pollyanna-type and misinformed statement. Pity is sent to those who do not want to trust in loving ways, in Godly ways." The following message was then issued.

*　　*　　*　　*　　*　　*

LEONARDO—

Lo and behold, you have touched an area of concern. We find it factually frustrating that the nemesis of peace is often caused by a lack of understanding what the true will of God really is. It is His intention now, and from the Creation of man, that all people are seen as equal in rights, in might, and in the reception of rewards. These are the cycles of belonging to a race [all mankind] that was formed to be a sharing and caring society.

Along the path of evolution, stories of despair, rather than stories of riches, began to be spread across the lands. Men decided that only certain distinctions of people were entitled to massive amounts of wealth; and so began the class system. It was at this unstated time that people began to feel as though they were not worthy of the same rewards as others. It is also what has created the feeling of distrust and anger that has led to clashes throughout the world. Violence has been born out of desperation when no desperation was warranted. If knowledge of the level of the infinite desires for all to have everything was understood, then there would never have been a reason for envious thoughts to have excelled to the level it has. People who have less than others continue to wallow on that path because they have let the misconceptions of abundance permeate their minds.

As you can see, just by this statement, being unaware of the virtues of greatness that God has cast upon all people, struggles will always continue. This is exactly why you need to remodel yourselves on a cellular level. In other words, you must begin to take time to examine the cause and affect for your actions. If you are already doing well in **all areas of life**, stay the course. On the other hand, if you aren't doing as good as you would like to in the matters of wealth, health, and overall happiness, then you are a perfect candidate to restructure the lessons imbedded in your mind and body.

No longer should the ideas of positive assimilation to higher aspects of life remain a secret. Share with your families and your friends all that you are learning. By staying true and honest to the idea that you can retrain your bodies and mind, immediate improvements will begin to unfold. It is also important for you to note that it might take some time for everything you want to be received. Even though life is abundant and infinitely secure, the human mind needs time to learn that it is completely all right to deal with it. It takes time to modify your development. Be patient, but be trusting of this most important message. God has given you the tools for inspiration and success!

*   *   *   *   *   *

Life works best when we manifest and see value in everything.

*   *   *   *   *   *

In going through some old papers, not coincidentally, I stumbled upon this next segment. It is largely intact from the original message. Deleted were some repetitive references to what you just read. One of the things I always find interesting is the consistent signs that Spirit gives when they want a particular point of view of a message to come across. The name of the spirit speaking was not given to me.

*   *   *   *   *   *

UNKNOWN SPIRIT— MENTAL PROSPERITY

The subject of prosperity for the mind is similar to understanding the riches that are within it. There is no function on earth that does not require a thought from your brain. Spirit works its wonders, normally through the use of electrical impulses. This is the form of energy that humans use as the brain signals all other aspects of the physical body. While it is important to have intelligence, it means nothing when concerning the mind. Spirit sees the mind and brain as two separate entities. Within the mind you need not be bright, from an intellectual standpoint, but you do need to understand that Spirit helps all people seem bright because of the Light of God. This is regardless of their aptitude, from genius to idiot. Spirit allows you to understand anything in a very realistic way. It is a gift for you.

All of you are being pressed by certain situations. It makes each of you wonder what to do next. For some, it is romantic or work-related concerns; for others, it may be health or financially related. All in all, the answers come from within the mind, where the abundance can work its magic. Vibrations are felt and then stimulate sectors of the body for maximum operation. The value of having mental prosperity is so that you understand what to do in day-to-day situations. Feeling trapped at any time will do nothing but wear on you and depress you. The prosperity I speak of is infinite intelligence. It allows anyone who is looking for positive things to create them with more ease than they thought possible.

For those who can physically [or psychically] see images, you must begin to interpret what you see. Some of you who hear Spirit must also do this, as must those of you who sense. If you feel you fall into none of these categories, Spirit wishes to inform you that you are able to channel inwardly. There is a knowledge that is derived from your souls' past lives. This intelligence can be tapped from within yourself, from that energy center, rather than from the sources outside your body. This is what makes many people confused as far as their psychic abilities. Sometimes there is no need for further development because the soul has lived and learned so many times before. All of that information is stored within the confines of yourself.

This inherited intelligence is easily accepted and does not need to be transmitted from the outer realm of spirit. People who seem to envision next to nothing are able to pull so much information from their own soul that the darkness that they see is unimportant, spiritually speaking.

Mental prosperity also comes to you so that you can learn, not only about your actions, but also about life's actions. As you continue to progress, you realize that all of the earth is intertwined and that nothing can be touched or left untouched that does not have a ramification on the future of many other things. A simple leaf falling off a tree fertilizes the ground. In turn, that feeds the insects, which, in turn, feed the birds, and the general process of evolution continues. While this leaf falling may seem insignificant to the average person, it also creates an opening for newer, healthier growth for the tree itself.

A refurbishment of life—and perhaps that is what you must understand—is that within your own mental capacity, you have the ability to change or redirect every aspect all the time, in all situations. There is no reason for you to languish in misery, when the propensity of thoughts from the mind and the rational reactive intelligence of the brain can create any growth and abundance you want. This is one of the best facts for you to remember.

*   *   *   *   *   *

Rejoice the time when land was seen as sacred and people were seen as equal. Rejoice the time when land was seen as sacred and people were seen as adversaries, for without this balance, we would not grow.

*   *   *   *   *   *

Perhaps more than anything, the empowerment Spirit gives us can be easily felt if you make an effort **not to fight** the changes that are necessary. I can only speak directly for myself, but there are days when my frustration, with what feels like a lack of progress, causes me to deny the messages and requests from the other side. After I flounder for a while, my stubbornness subsides and a rebalancing takes place. Life feels easier—at least until the next time my mood returns to the pull of wanting to do everything *my* way. It amazes me how often I disrupt the pattern of my life because I think I can do a better job if things go according to my own theories.

Ultimately, an acceptance of the Higher Self is truly the best way to move through our everyday existence. If we continue to try to exterminate the purest energies and help that is available, it is only fair that we have a harder time in life. On the other hand, absorbing the love, tranquility, purity, and peace that is available not only gives us a sense of overall empowerment, but it also makes us feel like we are invincible in administering our every positive whim and desire.

At one of my recent prayer and meditation group meetings, I was feeling somewhat stressed during the time everyone was in their own connection to Spirit. One of the things running through my mind was what balance does God and Spirit have when connecting to individuals.

They very simply said to me, "Whether an avatar or novice, the voice of God can be heard and felt. All people are treated equally."

I heard that and was once again reminded that we are truly never completely alone in our thoughts. It was one of the strongest surges of energy given to me in quite awhile. What I got most out of it was an empowering reminder that we are not destined to be frustrated and disillusioned. We are meant to embrace our Higher Purpose. This comes when we systematically infuse the wisdom given to us on so many different levels of life. Most of the choices I now make are increasingly attuned to the variety of subtle messages that God and Spirit give me. This is the same message that they want everyone to have. There is such a strong debt of gratitude that I feel for all the different entities that work with me. Even though I still run my life as a normal person—or as close to that as possible—I am never without the awareness of the great Presence that walks with me.

Many different types of messages were shared with you in this book. It is up to each of you to heed the advice, to take solace from the direction that Spirit is trying so repetitively to get all good people to absorb. If we listen to the stillness within a universe that has no stillness, you begin to comprehend that we are never as alone as we may feel. Spirit's main intention is to have all of us naturally embrace the pure qualities that make for an easier life.

Now that you have read and understand The Spoken Words of Spirit, don't be afraid to put them in motion. From personal experience, if you do, the internal peace that most of us strive for will come much easier. Love, financial success, and spiritual knowledge are available for all of us. Be a part of the greatness that is life. Grasp it readily, whether it's in big steps or small. You won't be sorry for expanding your mind to great new heights. I look forward to sharing with you more of the guidance from Spirit in the future.